BELOW
THE
WATERLINE

Best
Wirm

THE PLACE OF INFLUENTIAL POWER

BELOW THE WATERLINE

THOM WALTERS

TATE PUBLISHING
AND ENTERPRISES, LLC

Below the Waterline
Copyright © 2015 by Thom Walters. All rights reserved.

No part of this publication may be reproduced, stored in a retrieval system or transmitted in any way by any means, electronic, mechanical, photocopy, recording or otherwise without the prior permission of the author except as provided by USA copyright law.

This book is designed to provide accurate and authoritative information with regard to the subject matter covered. This information is given with the understanding that neither the author nor Tate Publishing, LLC is engaged in rendering legal, professional advice. Since the details of your situation are fact dependent, you should additionally seek the services of a competent professional.

The opinions expressed by the author are not necessarily those of Tate Publishing, LLC.

Published by Tate Publishing & Enterprises, LLC
127 E. Trade Center Terrace | Mustang, Oklahoma 73064 USA
1.888.361.9473 | www.tatepublishing.com

Tate Publishing is committed to excellence in the publishing industry. The company reflects the philosophy established by the founders, based on Psalm 68:11,
"The Lord gave the word and great was the company of those who published it."

Book design copyright © 2015 by Tate Publishing, LLC. All rights reserved.
Cover concepted and designed by Michael Henderson
Cover design by Nino Carlo Suico
Interior design by Manolito Bastasa

Published in the United States of America

ISBN: 978-1-68164-613-8
1. Business & Economics / Leadership
2. Business & Economics / Decision-Making & Problem Solving
15.07.23

Contents

INTRODUCTION

ONE AFTERNOON, DURING a tour of the Galapagos Islands, I took a break from snorkeling. I pulled myself out of the surf and stretched out on the subtle slope of the beach just beyond the breaking waves. The sand was firm but accommodating, and the intensity of the sun was balanced by gentle trade winds, making it perfect for soaking in the sun and observing my surroundings. I felt deep appreciation for the opportunity to experience this region of the world. The Galapagos, a chain of volcanic islands six hundred miles off the coast of Ecuador, have been protected through the intention and collaboration of the international community. Left untouched by commerce, they represent an authentic view of nature and the cycle of life.

Near where I sat, raucous colonies of sea lions covered the beach. Thousands of marine iguanas sunned on the black rocks, and to my excited delight, a baby sea lion chose to nap in the shade cast by my body—just two feet away.

Meanwhile, four large sea turtles made their way to the sea from the upper levels of the beach. With their size and armor-plated shells, they resembled small off-road vehicles. Eighty is considered middle-aged for these turtles, which filled me with a sense of wonder as I reflected on the deep understanding they must have of their environment.

Intent on getting to the water, they awkwardly navigated the peaks and valleys of the dunes. Their short legs sank into the sand as they rocked toward the shore with each intentional and forceful step. When they reached the edge of the sea, they slowed as they slipped into the surf, seemingly with a sense of relief, even though they were immediately tossed around on the waves. After bobbing around for a few moments, they slid with ease below the surface of the sea. They were graceful and fluid—a complete shift from their movements above the water. I moved closer to get a better view and noticed how effortless their movement seemed. They swam with intention amid the strong and shifting current, which I had experienced myself a short time earlier while snorkeling. Rather than fighting against the current, it seemed as if they were engaged in a playful and harmonious relationship with it—one they confidently knew.

A narrative unfolded for me in that moment, where the tension of the current wasn't something the turtles fought but rather something they joined with as though they were in partnership.

My experience with the sea turtles illustrates the subject of this book simply and clearly: the power of influence is the intention and ability to engage from a state of *being* versus a state of force or positional power. The turtles didn't struggle against the sea but moved into a relationship with it. They could ride the current and use it to support their efforts. Influence works similarly in terms of how we show up and interact with the world, where different outcomes are created when we have a clear and intentional way of showing up and *being* before doing.

I've been fascinated and drawn by the level of influence that can arise from simply being authentic and fully present in the moment, which is diametrically different from using positional power or force. I like to refer to these different approaches to influence as "below and above the waterline." Who we *are* exists below the waterline; what we *do* exists above the waterline. Above the waterline is what you do intellectually and technically—actions that are easy to see. Below the waterline is what you are made of, the experience you create—what other people feel, respond to, reflect on, and talk about. It's in the experience that shapes people's story of us.

Each of us is presented with moments in life where we become aware of when to take a new approach, where we shift our awareness to intentionally create something different—a new experience. In those moments we understand that something needs to unfold, something different from what has typically occurred in similar situations. We realize with clarity and purpose that we need to show up grounded and centered in our values, with courage and intention for what we want to accomplish. The situation might require that we be strong, kind, generous, light-hearted, patient, direct, discerning, playful, or any other way of being. When we have the clarity to recognize what's needed in the moment and intentionally shift to a state of being before doing, we can powerfully alter the situation. It is like the laws of physics at work—you can't see the formulas, but they change the environment. You too can be an alchemist of change.

I've always been fascinated by success—real success, the kind that is transformative, memorable, and sustainable. Why do some people or companies excel while others experience mediocrity or, at best, unsustained success? How does one person build and maintain trust and loyalty with others, garnering support and collaboration for his or her efforts, while others struggle with repeating patterns of failed endeavors and strained relationships?

I started asking myself these questions when I was nineteen years old and working for a global airline. It was eleven years later, when I was leaving the airline industry, that I realized everything I had been doing, every project I worked on, every encounter with a colleague or customer had been influenced by these questions: What will make this a successful experience? How can I assure desirable outcomes? Those questions informed the next phase of my professional life, where I became a behavioral strategist around the human dynamics of business, facilitating change in organizational cultures and creating deeper connections between businesses and their customers.

Every person I've worked with—whether a company executive, a new grad going on his or her first job interview, or a parent navigating the confusing world of teenagers—wanted to develop more effective ways to influence the world around them, to learn the difference between positional power and real power, the power of being.

In both professional and personal situations, the most common questions people ask are, what do you think will make a difference? What is missing in this situation? This thinking inspires me because it comes from a deep desire to understand a situation and do something differently—two essential ingredients for change.

Learning about true influence is not complicated. It requires more courage than intellect, and it can be fun. The insights and principles that make situations shift to bring about positive momentum are far from new. In fact, they have been around for centuries, so they are truly time-tested.

As I reflected on the principles and concepts that I would put in this book, I thought about all the books I've read and have been asked about. Many insightful, deeply intelligent, and artfully written books strive to help pave the way on this journey called *being human*. However, many of these books actually complicate matters by encouraging individuals to be someone different from who they are. When we are not authentic, almost every experience becomes an intellectual pursuit plagued by self-judgment.

My intention is to offer clarity, connection, and accessibility for opportunities of living, working, and playing at the level of authenticity, below the waterline, just like the confident and engaged sea turtles. My ideas are not to test you but rather help you discover what lies beneath your surface.

The privilege of a lifetime is being who you are.

—Joseph Campbell

PERSPECTIVE ON INFLUENCE

Knowing others is intelligence;
Knowing yourself is true wisdom.
Mastering others is strength;
Mastering yourself is true power.

—Laozi, *Tao Te Ching*

I WAS ASKED to mediate a challenging three-day session with the administration of a health-care system and the union that represented its nursing and allied health professionals. I spent the better part of that first day thinking I would not have believed what was unfolding if I were not seeing and hearing it firsthand.

Meredith, a senior administrator, started the session with a surprising and personally disclosing statement. Prior to the meeting that day, she said she had been reflecting over her career—specifically which interactions she was most proud of and which ones she wasn't proud of. Rather than elaborate on her past successes, she talked about her failures and how she was committed to not repeating them this week. One of her insights was how she and her team, with the union, had the opportunity to conduct these sessions differently from what they had done before and potentially build a partnership that would assure success across the system. She said to Trever, the union leader, "I'm sure it must be exhausting for you to be part of a polarized dynamic rather than one that feels like a partnership." Meredith commented that she was committed to openness, directness, and unfiltered curiosity (her exact words); and she hoped for their joint effort in creating an alignment that would really serve the system, its employees, and its members. She asked Trever and his team if there was anything she could do to make the process more effective. She would do her best over the next few days.

I watched with a level of awe as Trever palpably relaxed and referred to her by her first name. Rather than share war stories of the past, they talked about the future of health care and the need for increased collaboration at all levels to address quality and efficiency issues. They talked about how they might collaborate on staff development to close the divide and start creating a culture of alignment.

At the end of the first day, I overheard Meredith ask about Trever's grandmother, who had just lost her husband of sixty-three years. I felt so much respect for Meredith and her choice to make that an intimate moment at the end of the day rather than an emotional posturing at the beginning of the meeting.

After two days of observing this eloquent, confident, and very human administrator engaged with this union leader and his team, I asked Meredith what went on for her during these discussions. She said, "I told myself to let go and be present. I'm done with complicating things. I decided to be open to the possibilities instead of assume what would happen." She commented as we were walking out of the room that she knew this could be easier and that they could get better results over the long term if they really were partnered going forward. "Something else happened for me early the first day of the session," she said. "I realized that this is the person I set out to be when I got into my profession, and this is how I want to show up in the world. Instead of feeling stressed and tired, I feel calm, actually energized and confident about our future—even though we have a lot of work ahead of us." I said to her, "I'm going to quote you word for word on that."

Five years after those series of meetings, I received a notice from Meredith's assistant sharing news that Meredith was being recognized as one of the most influential and innovative leaders inside a seven-state health-care system. She was described as a person who brought down walls and built bridges to connect the present to the future.

Influence is frequently confused with positional power or stature and can be regarded as a type of force. I sometimes hear influence described as a sophisticated way to get people to do what you want—basically finding creative and socially acceptable ways to manipulate. This model of influence can embody everything from outright manipulation to more subtle ways of controlling people's behavior. This approach to influence requires constant efforts to keep people going in the direction you want and increasing levels of pressure to deal with the resistance and conflict that arise. Also, people spend inordinate amounts of time and energy to justify and defend their positions, which further confuses and polarizes interactions.

We are deeply in need of an authentic form of influence today, one that comes from first *being* then doing. States of being come from a focused clarity about who you are, including the core set of uncompromising values that define you, and how you choose to show up in any moment—basically the experience you want to create with people. In a state of being rather than doing, you are centered in a clear intention of creating meaning and connection in what you do. There's no need to justify this state of being or to defend it—you just need to show up for it, and that action and intention creates connection and unifies trust and commitment. For me, this means never sending someone away less than who she was when she entered my presence. If possible, I will send him away more than he was when we first connected with each other.

Influence is the ability to move mountains without the use of stature or force. This kind of influence creates an arresting form of presence because it is confident, clear, focused, and engaging. It resonates a powerful level of trust, and no one would think to manipulate it. Here's a wonderful and simple way to consider what I'm talking about: Imagine the conversation or thought that would take place about you when you leave a room. Would that conversation or thought lift your confidence? Or would it make you feel anxious and insecure? Does it resonate with respect and trust?

When we approach influence by *doing* rather than *being*, the focus is on coercing, manipulating, or forcing what we want out of other people or situations. While this approach can achieve the things we want in the short term, it can also disconnect us from our true values and impact trust, credibility, and ultimately, the outcomes we most desire.

Below and above the waterline is a mental model for recognizing and naming the power of being versus doing. In the world of business we reference this difference between how a company is perceived and what a company does. What a company does lives in its business strategy; how a company is perceived lives in its *brand*. How people feel and talk about the company is also known as its reputation.

Individual people and organizational leadership teams who view their power above the waterline behave in interesting and observable ways. When these people get into a situation that they know is a mistake or that has negative ramifications, they try to justify or manipulate their way out of the predicament. Similarly companies try to advertise or PR their way out. These individuals definitely get movement, but at the same time, they keep losing credibility, loyalty, and influence. Make no mistake about what I am saying. There is nothing wrong with doing and achieving. Doing and achieving help make up the fabric of our lives and are very much one of the ways we put our energy and commitment into the process of life. However, the moment we start to believe that what we *do* is who we are or that our power lives in what we do and achieve, we become disconnected from our true power and connected to a fallacy that moves us further from what really makes us credible and brilliant.

We are going through an era of profound change in which people question many belief systems that have previously been casually accepted. This change, or transformation, is different from the change brought about by the technical and scientific breakthroughs of previous decades. This new era of change affects all aspects of our lives— personal relationships, organizational cultures, consumer groups, and global communities.

We are emerging from an old paradigm based on force. The old paradigm story is about outsmarting, manipulating, deceiving, bartering, and trading our way to where we are today: eroded confidence and trust in traditional institutions and their leaders, broken personal relationships, failed communities, and unsustainable efforts to resolve, innovate, and transform important societal concerns such as health, education, and energy. Force, as the main character in this story, creates opposition, and its effect is to polarize rather than unify. The main themes in this old story are scarcity, separation, control, fear, obfuscation, and unhealthy competition. And how does this story end? With individuals being disconnected from who they are capable of becoming with no understanding of how to show up and influence and transform the world around them.

The paradigm of authentic, influential power is qualitatively different from the paradigm of force. This paradigm has a narrative of courage, clarity, confidence, and trust, which promotes meaning, connection, progression, resolution, and success of the whole, of all the entities involved. (When I use the term *narrative*, it means the story or meaning behind something.) The core differentiator of authentic, influential power is that this state of being is guided not by regulations or dictates but rather by principles—in other words, standards. Principles are not abstract and ethereal but rather concrete organizing values that create context and guide actions, rules, and behaviors. For example, an act of humanity that is carried out by a person based on his or her underlying values or guiding principles is a response from who that person is versus a set of rules he or she is following. We see many examples of this around the world and in our daily lives—people acting with open generosity of intention, helping others in need, working to innovate a situation, or inspiring another person's ability.

A simple example to understand principles and how they guide our actions is to consider the act of stealing. Do you not steal because the law says not to steal? Or do you not steal because you live by a set of principles that makes stealing a violation of your personal values? When you think about aligning with your authentic power, an intentional way of *being*, you can immediately feel challenged by what this would mean for you. You could be tempted to get overwhelmed or fall into cynicism and apathy, thinking the way things have been is just going to be the way they are.

Pause.

You also know that the implications and cost of continuing to live under the old paradigm are too great in all aspects of your personal and professional life. Imagine widespread societal change to a paradigm that is guided by principles. It's here, and it's growing.

Real change—the kind of substantive, sustainable change that we keep looking for—will not be achieved by altering superficial actions and behaviors. These tactics never go deep enough or offer real transformation. We, as individuals, are the influential agents of this change. As we strive to create a paradigm that feels different, sounds different, looks different, and *is* different, we will be operating from a place of shifting focus. We need to shift from a singular, linear, and rote focus of doing to a more expansive place of being and integrating our true selves—the space below the waterline. This shift represents a reconnection to a higher level of awareness, insight, confidence, integrity, and true power.

The power of this kind of authenticity is simply stated on a bumper sticker I saw: Think Globally, Act Locally. It's a profound statement of possibility because it exposes a relevant truth: it all starts with me. Everything you do and all the people you affect—it all starts with who you are at the being level and how you choose to show up and engage.

We all know individuals who inspire us to act, who cause us to strive, whom we want to emulate, and whom we follow with confidence and trust. One thing these inspiring and memorable individuals have in common is this: We talk about who they are before we talk about what they do. We talk about them as real, bright, confident, fun, human, and trustworthy. These people function in the world with intention and purpose—they are clear, courageous, and *choiceful*. I use the word *choiceful* to emphasize the power of choice over the powerlessness of reaction. These individuals show us the difference between embracing being and getting lost in doing because they live and engage from a conscious choice versus an unconscious reaction. My first recall of a person like this was my grandfather. I didn't have the awareness as a preteen to describe the experience of him at that time. What was clear was how different I felt around him, and to this day, decades later and having only had him in my life for twelve years, his presence and words of confidence and insight still influence me.

In the realm of influence, leadership is an interesting topic. Leadership is one of the most valued human attributes, and it's one of the most mystifying. Many people believe that good leadership is divinely bestowed upon a select few. A multitude of books on leadership tell you how to be more like someone else and less like yourself. It's compelling to step beyond the hype to look at the really good leaders over a period of time. How have they been influential? What is most remembered? What is it about them that captures the hearts and minds of individuals—whether family, friends, acquaintances, customers, colleagues, or employees?

People are eager to develop their own potential as leaders and authentic beings, as evidenced by the burgeoning "coaching" industry. People are seeking out life coaches and mentors and paying for their services to help facilitate self-discovery and development of authentic, personal power to influence change.

When we develop the insight and capacity for being versus doing, we begin to differentiate between a transaction and an experience. When we are lost in doing, others experience us as a transaction, one that is neither memorable nor influential. When we are focused first on being, we create an experience that others walk away remembering and talking about. It is not difficult to live this way, and it does not take years to achieve. Yes, it is challenging, and it takes courage because it requires us to be real, present, and intentional—to be aware. But when you violate your own principles of truth, integrity, and courage for convenience, you actually relinquish great power.

Tips for Your Development

My intention is to offer perspective as you uncover your own authentic influence and what it means to differentiate between being and doing. The principles and concepts in this book offer a context and a framework for accessing and developing your insight, capacity, and power for being.

As humans, we are uniquely developmental. We change, grow, and expand our capacity for being and doing. However, growth generally only happens when conditions are just right. Here are a few qualities I believe are critical for success in developing commitment and acumen with the concepts outlined in this book.

- ○ You must have a desire for personal development and an awareness of your own growth. You might say, "It's great that I'm not a finished product, and I will never stop developing and growing."

- You must have a commitment to personal integrity, the desire/intention to act from a place of personal values and accountability at all times—not just when it's convenient.
- You must exercise courage. Challenge yourself to act in the face of anxiety or fear with integrity and intention. Fear is a slippery slope that can distort the facts and cause you to get lost in confusion, reaction, and passiveness.
- You must be curious. Have a desire to learn more about something you already know, as well as the things you don't know. Be open and don't resist things you've not experienced or things that make you uncomfortable.
- You must develop a connection with something that grounds you in your humility. Explore ideas, inter-personal dynamics, or activities that pull you out of your ego. Get real and stay real.
- You must foster lightheartedness. Don't take yourself so seriously.

CREATIVE TENSION

*The things we fear most—fluctuations, disturbances,
imbalances—are the primary sources of creativity.*

—Margaret Wheatley

STEPHANIE WAS A participant in a leadership retreat I was facilitating. She said during a breakout session, "I really want to have a chance to direct one of the client projects at my company. I feel ready, and I know I would do an amazing job." I asked her what was keeping her from pursuing it. She paused and replied, "I don't know if my boss would be supportive, and he would need to find a replacement for my position." I asked her what kept her from sitting down to explore this with her boss. "I'm afraid," she said with a deep breath.

At the end of the session I asked the participants what their key takeaways were and the next steps they would pursue based on the session. "I've already done it." Stephanie grinned. She had called her boss during the break to set up a meeting. "I had to step into the moment while it was in front of me rather than continue to overthink it." Three months later she got a client project to lead, and I heard from her boss some time later that Stephanie was the second runner-up to lead the new office in the United Kingdom. Her boss went on to say, "Even though she didn't get that position, she will be leading an office in the next year or two. I know it."

There is a universal force that touches every aspect of our lives, and it knows no boundaries. Known as *creative tension* among leading thinkers on the subject of change, this phenomenon explains what motivates people to make changes in their lives or develop themselves. Creative tension is the dynamic that is present when we recognize the difference between where we are and where we want to be or the gap between our current situation and our desired situation. We may react or respond to this dynamic gap by being aware of it and trying to understand it or becoming uncomfortable and wanting to avoid it.

The gap is the distance between what we have and what we want or the space that exists before we embrace an opportunity or pursue a possibility. This space creates a healthy tension that seeks to resolve itself, and the tension is the reason choices are made and actions are taken. It's the source of energy for all change and growth. Creative tension is also present in the natural laws of the universe. It's the energy that makes things change, grow, and shift. This influence can be seen in the fields that study living systems such as biology, physiology, and psychology.

Our daily lives contain many instances of creative tension. Remember the anxiety and excitement about whether to kiss your date the first time? That's creative tension. As an athlete or a performer, the tension before a game or a performance that makes you wonder what you are capable of—creative tension. When you ask your daughter who was in the car with her when she had a fender bender and she pauses to decide how honest to be—creative tension. In that meeting when you wanted to look and sound smart to impress your colleagues and considered whether to say something or continue to listen—creative tension. When a stressed client is critical of the time line you gave him and you think of whether to defend yourself or ask questions to understand his concern—creative tension.

Some of you may already be aware of this dynamic and have an astute understanding of how it plays out in your life. Some of you may know when and how to step into it and embrace it as an opportunity rather than seeing it as an obstacle that needs to be resisted. Many people don't understand it, but they are familiar with the discomfort. These people can quickly become resistant, defensive, or reactive when this dynamic appears.

Creative tension is like the law of gravity: you know it's there, but you rarely think about it. With awareness, creative tension can be harnessed and engaged—or avoided. When you avoid it, opportunities are missed and situations go from being creative to becoming more tense, which can become increasingly chaotic and, over time, destructive and toxic.

Let's pause a moment.

I want to really ground you in the significance of this dynamic: The ability to consciously recognize creative tension when it is present is the center of learning to engage and influence situations from small to significant—within yourself and as you interact with others. The effort you put into recognizing and embracing this power will move you to profound levels of growth and influence in your life. I want to highlight this as you will most likely experience creative tension through the other chapters of this book. So watch for the resistance or frustration when it appears and explore it. The resistance, or what I like to call the *thrash*, is normal, and we all go through it as we wake up and become aware of our patterns and become courageous with our personal growth.

Let's continue.

Everyone is familiar with tension, and most of us would describe it as a negative experience. It can create undesirable emotions and bring out our worst characteristics. Creative tension signals that a moment has shifted and we now face something that falls outside our previous experience or comfort zone. The most common feelings we experience when creative tension comes up are degrees of anxiety, fear, or internal defensiveness. Frequently some excitement will accompany the anxiety if we view the situation as an opportunity.

The discomfort is not good or bad; it simply indicates that a shift has occurred. In these moments of opportunity, we face choices. The challenge or opportunity is to recognize the discomfort as a point of growth and development, not as something bad that needs to be avoided. Our heightened protective reactions, sometimes referred to as our fight or flight response, have conditioned us to become defensive when we feel uncomfortable instead of becoming curious. These finely tuned protective instincts are important in life-threatening situations. However, the creative tension we are exploring here does not fall into survival or life-and-death experiences—although sometimes it feels that way. Thank you, ego.

In any given situation, when we pause with curiosity, we are able to connect through awareness and consciously choose what we want to do with the situation or opportunity. By accessing your own awareness, you ground yourself in reality rather than projection and can step forward with the power of intention. This word *intention* is important to grasp because it is a very powerful state of clarity. It's a goal or aim that guides your thoughts, attitudes, choices, and activities. Make no mistake—intentions influence your actual experiences. Intention is one of the most powerful centering points one can use in all situations.

Creative tension is ever present when you need to have an important or challenging conversation with your boss, your colleague, your parents, your son or daughter, your client, or your partner or spouse. These conversations require you to be honest and may need you to address something that is uncomfortable. Creative tension is not always associated with situations we perceive as problematic. Often creative tension is related to pursuing something that we desire but fear we are not good enough to get, such as a professional or personal opportunity. The creative tension provides an opportunity for you to declare what you want and have a real conversation about it. It is a clarifying catalyst that will mobilize you to go after your desires with intention or identify where and why you are holding back.

Avoiding Creative Tension Is Oh So Obvious

When I spend time inside any organization, I can quickly tell whether or not the company has developed a capacity for engaging creative tension. In organizations that avoid creative tension, the culture has an appeasing dynamic about it, where it avoids rather than engages and challenges when things don't work. Leadership in these organizations typically resists change and often expends energy and time reacting to it. They have a difficult time knowing the difference between priorities and distractions and frequently avoid making trade-off decisions. They struggle to break free from the status quo to embrace innovation and are more likely to add new window dressing to old habits or create more layers of bureaucracy to deal with unresolved issues.

When working with an executive group, it generally becomes apparent to me pretty quickly if they are a team that embraces creative tension. If they are, they usually exhibit commitment and focus on developing a strong and engaged leadership team that reflects high levels of accountability, transparency, real-time communications, and collaborative relationships—overall higher levels of credibility and trust. These leadership teams tend to be more confident and aspirational. They distill better ideas and adapt to change more readily and successfully, and they are more trusted and influential mentors to direct reports.

When I avoid creative tension in important areas of my own life, anxiety starts to rise, resentment might filter through, and courage falls. Every time I'm giving a talk or teaching a seminar, I feel a palpable level of creative tension before I step in front of the audience. I use that energy to center and focus myself, and it keeps me real, which the audience connects with. What does the energy feel and sound like? I'm aware that I feel a sense of vulnerability by stepping in front of the audience, so I acknowledge, "Wow, that amazing feeling of vulnerability, that's the human part of me." The other part is knowing, not questioning, that I am smart and have something to offer and I'm going to have fun with the audience. I don't need to pretend to be someone but am able to be myself.

The Force Is with Us

I've come to describe *creative tension* as a force, an energy or awareness that grabs you. There is no mistake about its presence, but it never draws blood. It can be experienced as anxiety or excitement—or a combination of both.

When we face creative tension, our tendency most frequently is to overuse our intellect. We get lost in our linear and analytical thinking and can completely miss the opportunity in front of us. We may use the defenses of our rationale to come up with convenient ways to avoid the discomfort. Or we may create a projection, which is a set of flawed assumptions about the situation or dynamic. This type of reactive thinking disconnects us from the possibility of engaging with something different or new. It causes us to get lost in old stories that frequently lack relevance in the moment. These old stories are basically insignificant history—what I like to think of as outdated. The core of understanding creative tension and embracing it lies in your ability to integrate your head and heart. I'm talking about the ability to ask yourself, What am I feeling? What am I thinking? What am I saying to myself about the person I'm dealing with, the situation I'm in, or even just about myself?

This level of awareness allows us to step into *being*—being grounded, being integrated, and being present. We first have the sensation of the tension, the experience of actually feeling it. We then can use our head to quickly assess what is happening and make a choice that allows us to mobilize our courage with the clarity to step forward and engage.

Creative tension is not something you master; it is something you engage, in the moment, when an opportunity is in front of you. As you recognize creative tension and step into it, you will develop amazing insight, understanding, commitment, and capacity. And it will always keep you humble, surprised, and most frequently delighted.

An important aspect of my work is about the application of creative tension to create change, stimulate development, and resolve issues. My intention is to apply creative tension to help you increase your curiosity about yourself, shift your awareness, and grow your ability to choose how you show up. Embracing creative tension will help you develop greater capacity to understand and use your emotions, which are paramount in your ability to act from a place of being—below the waterline. Embracing creative tension will also bring more joy, less pain, and less struggle.

Creative tension is not optional and will not be denied.
It is an equal-opportunity provider—everyone gets equal
access and equal impact. When you understand and start to
recognize creative tension and then engage the opportunities, you will be able to shape your environment, expand
ideas, heighten thinking, deepen relationships, influence
outcomes, and stimulate your own development, as well as
the development of others. In other words, you start creating different outcomes daily.

Tips for Your Development

Creative tension causes discomfort or anticipation. The
discomfort can be in the form of anxiety, apprehension, or
insecurity. The feeling of anticipation can be excitement
about the prospect of something unfolding or coming
forward. Becoming aware and tracking when you feel discomfort will help you understand how to make intentional
choices in the moment.

- What three areas do you think you most avoid when
  creative tension is present? For example, Do you
  avoid stepping forward to ask for what you need? Do
  you appease others and walk away frustrated and disappointed? Do you avoid telling the truth to people

of authority? Do you get critical, dismissive, impatient, or embarrassed when something catches you off guard rather than curious to explore it? Do you avoid healthy risks or opportunities?

○ What are the old narratives you rely on when you avoid creative tension? How do you behave when these dynamics (familiar patterns and scenarios) are at play? If you don't know or are struggling to answer these questions, watch yourself for a week with focused objectivity (nonjudgment) for situations or patterns.

○ When you are in the midst of creative tension and anxiety, or the lack of courage causes you to become defensive or avoid the situation, try to shift to curiosity. Curiosity offers a no-pressure way to explore the situation. It can help you understand your own reactions or expectations. Curiosity feels neutral and safe, and it has a subtle, detached lightheartedness.

Try these exercises:

○ When someone has expectations that are unclear or that make you anxious, ask for clarity rather than make assumptions or try to read the other person's mind: "To make sure I'm on the same page with you, it would be helpful for me to better understand _____."

- When someone is frustrated, take that as an invitation to find out what they need rather than ignore them or defend yourself. It can sometimes be useful to offer a bit of humor. In some intense situations, I've asked with a playful tone, "Would you like to talk about this, or would you like to keep dancing around me?" The other person usually laughs.

- If the creative tension diminishes the confidence you need to do something, be generous with yourself and ask for some oversight, coaching, or examples. Ask for what you need to align with your confidence because confidence really allows us to excel. And actually people will respect you if you have the confidence to ask for what you need. Be sure to give context to your need so that the other person is not simply offering a solution. Sometimes we need clarity, insight, direction, context, resources, assistance, time, and feedback.

- I always keep three qualities at the forefront of my intentions, and when I am centered in these qualities, I know I can be present with creative tension:

- Courage. Courage is not the absence of fear or anxiety; it is the ability to move in the presence of it.
- Humanity. Always stay centered on your values. For me these are respect, honesty, fairness, humor, and patience.
- Lightheartedness. Lighten up the situation. Most things in life can be approached with blitheness and an unburdened attitude. Don't take yourself or the situation so seriously. Everyone else in the situation usually lightens up with you.

UNDERSTANDING VS. BEING RIGHT

*There is no more destructive force in human affairs—
not greed, not hatred—than the desire to have been
right. Nonattachment to possessions is trivial when
compared with nonattachment to opinions.*

—Mark Kleiman

FIVE PARTNERS IN a medical practice were stuck over the buyout terms in their partnership agreement. One of the partners wanted to leave the group, and if the terms of the agreement were followed as written, it would compromise the group financially to a point that could impact the group's stability. In addition, a noncompete clause would prevent the partner who wanted to leave from working in the region for three years.

The partners had several angry, argumentative meetings and then resorted to communicating only through their attorneys and written memos. I received a call from Stewart, one of the physician partners. He said he desperately wanted to salvage what seemed unsalvageable. He told me he believed the volatile and angry situation wasn't actually caused by the senior partner wanting to leave but stemmed from a long pattern of unhealthy behavior by the whole group. His partner's decision to leave had only brought it to the surface. He felt really anxious about whether individuals would even be willing to explore a resolution. He thought they might prefer to fight it out.

After spending a good forty-five minutes letting the group kick my tires and look under the hood to see if I was worth their time, we moved the conversation to a more practical focus. I told them I had two stipulations if I were to work with them: they could not have attorneys present, and they had to agree to stay for an entire weekend retreat away from the office. After a tense and defensive debate, they agreed to the retreat.

In discussions during our first afternoon of the weekend together, several needs arose. Al, the partner who wanted to leave, never felt appreciated by the others for what he had created in the partnership and for the consequent benefits the other partners received from it. He also resented that some of the partners had gone behind his back and discussed partnership problems with external constituents. He felt betrayed and embarrassed by this action.

The other partners felt they had been treated disrespectfully and had been unreasonably dominated and controlled by Al in his role as managing partner. Each of them cited individual examples in which Al had been rude or arrogant in his behavior. As a group they resented that he would make policy decisions affecting the partnership without discussing them with others. All of them, for different reasons, needed to feel respected and treated fairly. All of them also wanted to remain in the city and continue their practices; therefore, they needed to keep good professional reputations in the community.

By Friday evening, after four hours of awkward, tense, and emotionally draining discussions, I brought the session to a close. Saturday morning we regrouped. After casual chitchat about walks some had taken around the lake that morning, Stewart said he had something he wanted to share. He told the group in a calm, clear, and confident tone that he had been reflecting on Friday's conversation. He said the most significant thing to him was how he and the others spent more time blaming one another for issues rather than resolving them. He went on to say he felt ashamed of his own behavior and wanted to leave the weekend proud of his partners and reassured he had not lost his own integrity and character. He continued to tell the group how he used the conflict with his partners to build a case against Al and, over time, consumed by his own agendas, had come to treat his partners as commodities. Stewart then said, "We are greater people than this, and I for one want to ask your forgiveness and for you to tell me how I can rebuild your trust." I sat there with a deep sense of awe coming over me.

Kathryn, one of the partners, was the first to speak: "I'm sitting here feeling exposed as I reflect on my own behavior, and you, Stewart, have my profound admiration for your courage to do what you just did. You do have my trust and commitment." Stewart's comments cracked the group open to the most transparent and honest space with one another. They began sharing personal stories of themselves in a way they had never done before. They offered one another real insight into who they were as individuals. I watched as they listened and really explored one another's aspirations and concerns. The tenor of their voices changed. The pace and clarity of how they talked shifted, and they spent more time asking questions than making statements. I remember thinking, *Wow, if this could only be captured on video.* They spent the rest of the day fully engaged in talk-

ing about their lives and relationships and personal joys
and disappointments.

Sunday morning I felt excited and nervous, wondering if the romance had worn off and where the conversation might go. I opened the morning with recognition and
feedback of what occurred the day before. I shared with
them the deep character and willingness they had exhibited
individually to shift their posture and move to something
completely different. "Where would you like to go today?"
I asked. Mark, the youngest in the group, said he would
like to see the group talk about what the future might look
like. He emphasized the word *might*. He asked if I would
help the group play with possibilities without getting into
specific solutions. One of the breakthroughs during the day
was Al declaring he was planning to go to art school when
he left the group.

Everyone became clear on numerous desires and needs
and decided to set up several more planning sessions over
the next two weeks to craft a plan. They asked me to facilitate those meetings because they wanted to do this without
attorneys present. At the end of the second planning session (there were four scheduled), they came to an agreement. Al was going to stay with the group in a 60-percent
capacity and attend a two-year art-school program on his
days off. He would dissolve his partnership as part of a

transition plan and move to a contracted physician position with the group. The group would buy him out over a five-year period, which is how long he wanted to work.

The group asked Kathryn to be managing partner; she humbly and eagerly accepted.

In many situations we tend to operate from one of two postures: either we are trying to *understand* or we are trying to be *right*. When we try to be right, we start from a place of resistance. We've already formulated a perception, opinion, or judgment, which informs a position. Holding that position generally requires resistance, rigidity, control, defensiveness, and, at times, self-righteousness. When we are trying to be right, we invite reciprocating resistance and defensiveness from others—and we trigger their fear. Our rigid position, also known as defensiveness, typically stems from our unconscious fear.

When we try to understand, we suspend judgment, assumptions, perceptions, and defense, and simply focus on comprehension and integration of meaning. This level of intention to understand comes from a posture of openness, curiosity, and exploration. When we try to understand, we operate from a place of centeredness, confidence, and calm, which enables us to suspend reaction and get clarity. When we are in a posture of understanding, we are not caught in fear or lost in the pain of a perceived injustice. We may be aware of fear, but it does not dictate or control our capacity for choice and our ability to be fully present.

When we are in a posture of wanting to be right, we are plugged into our unconscious fear. It causes us to make assumptions and judgments, cling to prejudice, and become reactive and defensive.

The problem with trying to be right is that we create resistance, defensiveness, and conflict. In effect we end up being wrong because we lose our connection with others and our effectiveness at eliciting trust, cooperation, and commitment—our ability to be influential. We actually gain nothing, and we walk away from these interactions lost in the fantasy that we're powerful because we're not wrong. But oh so wrong and so lost we are!

The desire to be right is a source of significant conflict and suffering. This particular motivation isn't nearly as easy to identify as greed or hatred. Most people instinctively recognize the motive and attitude of needing to be right in others but struggle to recognize it in themselves. That's because it comes from that unconscious, patterned place.

When we are in a posture of wanting to be right, we cause others to constrict their thinking and, therefore, their ability to understand us. It also constricts their emotions and willingness to be generous with us. In other words, when I come at you in a posture of needing to be right—no matter how subtle I am—I automatically make you wrong, and it causes you to feel resistant or defensive. You then have the need to defend or justify your position, so rather than feeling open, generous, and engaging toward me, you feel closed off and guarded or defensive.

Trying to be right pushes people away from us instead of drawing them toward us. It gets us the exact opposite of what we really want, which is another's trust, connection, cooperation, and commitment.

When we are trying to be right, we withdraw to protect ourselves rather than come together to do what needs to be done. It happens every day in every organization. It happens every day in personal relationships. It happens every day between parents and children. It happens every day among people who encounter one another on the street.

When we try to be right with one another, we get stuck, defensive, pitted, and not committed to anything except being right.

We are trying to be right when we do the following:

- ○ Plan our defense while others are talking
- ○ Wear others down in an argument to prove our point
- ○ Stay tough and angry rather than attempting to resolve
- ○ Attempt to make others feel guilty and obligated as a way to get our way

- Use force, threats, or intimidation to get others to do what we want
- Use authority and position to overpower
- Use deception or fear to manipulate others
- Keep score to justify taking advantage of or deceiving others
- Shift the blame
- Refuse to be accountable for the impact of our behavior on others
- Use logical persuasion to convince others of something
- Overwhelm others with data and facts
- Become self-righteous and moralistic
- Claim to have someone else in authority on our side
- Become judgmental and critical
- Become superior and dismissive
- Do something ourselves to prove to others that we are better than they thought
- Do not believe that we can afford to listen

It is important that you recognize the unique behavioral patterns you display when you are trying to be right, which will offer important insights to help you shift your intention and position in those moments. These behavioral patterns usually live in the areas you feel most defended, reactive, or fearful.

Learning to shift in the moment from an unconscious, reactive position to a conscious one is powerful, and it is the first step toward being present and choiceful.

Recognizing your own patterns is not about judging what you see in yourself; rather, it's about using insight, some compassion, a bit of humor, and healthy doses of courage and integrity to shift and step into the posture of understanding. In this uncomfortable yet fantastic moment, pause to ask yourself, What is the fear or insecurity that drives my need to be *right* in this moment?

When you try to understand, you produce the opposite outcome from what happens when you try to be right. Others feel expansive around you—in their thinking as well as their emotions—and their ability to understand you increases. They are also more willing to be open and generous to a different point of view or activity.

Reflecting back on Stewart in the medical group, when he chose to get out of being right and defended and became authentic with the group, he shifted the pattern for the whole group, and people became conscious and accountable with their own patterns—they mirrored his courage.

When you try to understand, others feel safe and are more likely to take responsibility for their share of what needs to be done as well as for what does not work. Everyone becomes more willing to connect, trust, and commit. It builds capacity in others when they are open to taking risks and doing something different from what they might have imagined before. You open up a place of possibility.

The word *understand* has a depth of meaning beyond the definition most frequently used in our day-to-day exchange. When I say, "I understand," I could mean that I hear what you are saying literally and yet have no idea what it really means to you. To understand can be superficial and meaningless, or it can be relevant and life changing.

My definition of the word *understand* is the experience of being in a mental and emotional posture to comprehend, discern, empathize, and grasp meaning. To really understand causes a shift in me. It is different from just hearing the words spoken or sensing the emotions of another person. The ability to move into a posture of understanding means I am open and willing: I have the intention to suspend judgment or prejudice so I can hear, grasp, and discern what is happening around me or you. I am willing to push the pause button on my own mental chatter and really hear and comprehend what you are saying or doing. When I step into this level of intention, I shift from not being aware and having a fear of being out of control to a place of expansion, clarity, and calm. In this space I can connect and move things forward in a completely different way. This place is below the waterline.

Control Is a Fallacy

When we let go of our fear and insecurity, as well as of our projected stories and judgments, we can experience a brilliant point of awareness and courage. We begin to know with confidence that we give up nothing if we suspend our reactions and move into a posture of trying to understand. It becomes compellingly clear we gain a great deal and lose nothing—except perhaps some of our ego struggle and fear.

We have become so conditioned to the fallacy, the belief that someone is always right and someone is always wrong. It's incredible how much time and energy we spend judging circumstances and making sure "I am right" or at least "It's not me that's wrong." Breaking through this fallacy helps us let go of our *need to control*, which is brought on by the fear of losing power and the fear that somehow someone will take advantage of us or get the upper hand if we are not right. The overwhelming fear is of losing something, whatever it is (fill in the blanks) or, maybe worse, of being wrong. We carry a deep, unconscious, distorted defensiveness against being wrong. If we are right, we win; and if we are wrong, we lose. It becomes an all-or-nothing proposition.

Much of the restrictive, fear-based, even punitive doctrine that some of us grew up with encodes a black-and-white concept of being right or wrong. This creates distortion around right and wrong and pits people in a polarized world of either/or rather than a world that promotes understanding, new truths, connection, resolution, and new beginnings. At the core of this distortion is the fear of being out of control, being judged and rejected—being wrong.

The polarization makes us want to protect and defend our position. We feel a need to judge, assign blame, separate, punish, and ultimately, reject others. In this space we are unaware of context and meaning, and we are disconnected from our humanity.

Pivoting with awareness in the face of fear and our projections to proceed with courage and a desire for clarity creates a new level of possibility and choice. The choice, in that moment, is how we will show up and engage. When our intention is to try to understand, we come with awareness of our own presence, our thinking, our emotions, and what we are bringing or not to the dynamic. The term *projection* is a slippery defense response. It's when we attribute to other people our own unacceptable emotions, thoughts, or experiences. For example, I might say, "He is angry with me" when in fact I'm angry with him.

Fear can create an interesting power play. When we act defensively and take on a posture of blaming others, we irrationally think we have scared away whatever it was that we feared, which then gives us a false and distorted sense of power. As an example, there is an attempt to give me some performance feedback, and it triggers fear in me—fear of criticism or judgment—so I immediately shift the focus off me and start blaming a member of the team whom I feel is not supportive of me. That team member is neither part of the topic nor relevant to my performance issues.

Do You Feel the Tension?

About now, you might be saying, "Thom, some people really are wrong, and certain things are wrong too. How can you say that it's not about right and wrong?"

When I talk about the difference between trying to understand and being right, I'm not talking about the atrocities committed against individuals and humanity or the hubris brought about by corruption. Acts of violence, cowardice, and greed are deep moral offenses and create great outrage to our sense of ethical and moral behavior. I'm talking instead about 90 percent of the experiences we have in life through our interactions with family members, colleagues, direct reports, bosses, clients, customers, and the person standing in line ahead of us. I am talking about the dynamics and interactions that make up most of our daily lives.

Your partner or spouse forgot to pick up the cleaning or was late to your child's soccer game. Your colleague forgot to include you in the meeting to prep for the client presentation. The client didn't give you credit in front of his boss for the work you did on the marketing plan. You show up on the wrong date for an appointment and are convinced the scheduler wrote the wrong date. A stranger cut in front of you at the barista counter. All these scenarios, these interactions trigger us. They can feel like assaults to our values and our sense of self-respect. Rather than petty inconveniences, they become moral offenses that make us begin to feel indignant or defensive.

I also understand that other debate going on in your head right now: "But sometimes I am right, Sometimes my spouse/partner/boss is wrong." Yes, you might be technically correct in the facts. You might feel like you have the moral edge in your rightness because of poor judgment, disorganization, or lack of fairness on someone else's part. Yes, someone may have engaged you in something that felt disrespectful to you. Someone may have misunderstood you and jumped to inaccurate conclusions. Someone might have forgotten you. The moment that the feeling of "rightness" comes over you, you may be technically correct in your data or in terms of the experience you had. However, rarely will you be recognized for your rightness. What's at stake here is not the accuracy of your data or your judgments or your perceptions. What's at stake is your ego (that unconscious part of you) getting bruised and needing to defend and justify. It's that part of us that fears we are not seen or validated.

Our ego feels like fragile territory, where fears of being taken advantage of are activated, and the only way to soothe it is to feed the craving for *recognition* related to a perceived offense. The fear present in these moments provides an opportunity for us to pivot into awareness and shift from the old narrative of perceived powerlessness to a new narrative of authentic power. That moment is where we consciously step into choice: I can choose to defend or choose to engage. I can choose to be right or choose to create understanding.

Let's pause for just a moment.

Take a deep breath. What I've been talking about is loaded with creative tension—or the not-so-subtle point of clarity when profound learning can occur. These moments give us an opportunity to move from being unconscious about something to being conscious. We begin to see clearly and can connect the dots in the larger picture. We grasp the consequences of behavior, and we sense the power of intention. In these moments we can pivot in that clarity and shift to a place of *being* versus a place of *reaction.*

It can be challenging to get the rational, literal part of our brain around this principle. It is hard to look beyond the defense that keeps us from seeing our behavior patterns and the fallacy of needing to be right.

When I first learned about this principle, I was twenty-nine. I understood the basic premise intellectually, but then the ego battle started—in other words, my fear and insecurity of being exposed and not being right reared its head. I was deeply afraid of the idea that "being right" could be insignificant. My sense of self-righteousness flared up, and I started a mental and emotional thrash that lasted for many weeks as I came to terms with the intensity of not wanting to be wrong. In full disclosure, I had, like most people, patterned ways of being right; and as I started to recognize them and not run from them, I felt an initial discomfort and embarrassment as I let the truth surface.

My finely tuned patterns of being right had served me well, so I liked to think. I was prone to overwhelming people with intellectual data, trying to outsmart people. I was skilled at being tough and independent: "I can do this on my own." Around the same time I received painful and overwhelming feedback from several colleagues and two close friends about how critical, dismissive, and faintly judgmental I could be. When people didn't quite measure up, I could let them know it in subtly critical ways or overwhelm them with my insights on how to do it better, which meant *my* way.

I remember the day my resistance lifted, the thrashing calmed, and the embarrassment turned to laughter. I felt this curiosity and awareness come over me. I suddenly got it! I felt like I had just been given a huge gift. I was like an excited kid as I talked with my mentor about the insight and power of this principle of *understanding*. "This will change my life," I said. He smiled, and I could see the recognition in his eyes when he said, "Now you will spend the rest of your life fine-tuning it."

This principle creates tension in many people's minds and emotions as they start to grapple with their own patterns of needing to be right and how they go about making others be wrong.

Let's take another moment so you can explore what it means to take on a posture of understanding.

What is percolating in you right now? What are you saying to yourself about what you just read, about your own patterns? Shift your thoughts and feelings away from judgments about the behavior patterns you may identify within yourself. What are you protecting, and what is your biggest fear? Is it that I'm not smart enough, creative enough, good enough, strong enough, or any other *enough*? What would happen if you let yourself off the hook and found some humor in your old patterns of wanting to be right?

If you are experiencing resistance, answer one question: What is the fear behind the resistance? What feels scary about acknowledging your patterns or in finding a bit of humor in the discovery? Most of us are afraid of being broken. If we acknowledge our patterns of needing to be right, then somehow we automatically admit to being wrong about that one thing. And being wrong has a broken quality to it. The simple truth is it's time to let go of being right and enjoy the reality that you are neither broken nor fixed. You are in the process of becoming more of who you are.

An important step to take as you develop a capacity for shifting into understanding is to identify and practice it with yourself. If you can't be open with yourself, it will be extremely difficult to be open with the world around you. I use curiosity and humor to do this with myself. Curiosity and humor are open emotional spaces and allow you to play or explore something, which means to take the test out of it: "Am I going to do it right or wrong?" This shifts the tone of the internal voice and opens up a level of mental clarity and emotional confidence that actually provides me with beneficial insight. And this insight usually inspires me to do something different from what I had previously been doing. I use this in every aspect of my life: professionally with clients, with personal and family relationships, and with the brief encounter with a stranger.

> *Shallow understanding from people of good will is more frustrating than absolute misunderstanding from people of ill will. (Martin Luther King Jr.)*

How to Make It Safe for Others by Shifting Your Posture to Understanding

An amazing aspect of our humanness is our ability to take risk, open ourselves, and connect when we feel safe. When I use the word *safe*, I don't mean physical safety but rather emotional safety—when we trust, we will not be taken advantage of or be inappropriately vulnerable. It's when you feel like you can do anything. You don't feel limitations, and you don't hold back. You step forward and embrace the moment.

Approaching a situation in a way that makes it safe *for others* fosters awareness in oneself in the moment. It enables us to shift our position away from being right and become centered in our true intentions for how we'd like an interaction to go with another person or group. For example, "I would like to make it easy for this person to trust me, collaborate with me, have fun, and be accountable, generous, and honest."

Create an environment of safety for others:

- Listen and try to understand.*
- Don't plan your defense while another person is talking.
- Consider whether the other person needs to look good for some reason or to some other person. Send him or her home a hero.
- Don't ask rhetorical questions that make others feel the need to justify themselves. Rhetorical questions usually begin with *why* and have an implied *stupid* at the end. "Why did you do that, stupid?" Ask questions of genuine curiosity: "Can you explain that to me so I can connect the dots? Help me understand how that came about—I'm confused."
- Begin the conversation trusting.
- Listen and try to understand.*

---

* A not-so-subtle reminder!

○ Don't argue about who did what in the past or who's at fault. Instead focus on whether there is a reason to have a future relationship, what characteristics you both would like that relationship to have, and what you are willing to commit in order to make it happen.

○ Explore with the other person the possibility of a more respectful and open dialogue between the two of you.

○ Focus on analyzing the problem and understanding and accepting everyone's underlying needs and objectives.

○ Listen and try to understand.*

○ Engage by advocating and partnering rather than passively observing and critiquing.

○ Choose to be appropriately vulnerable. Tell others what you know. Tell them what you think and assume. Tell them how their behavior impacts your relationship. Tell them what you need.

○ Listen and try to understand.*

○ Surprise others by not living up to their worst expectations of you. If they expect you to be loud, be quiet. If they expect you to bully them, be gentle. If they expect you to be dramatic, be low-key. If they expect you to storm out, stay put. If they expect you to not say anything, talk. You may surprise yourself as well as others. When one person shifts, so will the others, in most cases.

- ○ Listen and try to understand.*
- ○ Be generous. Generosity begets generosity.
- ○ Be aware and accountable for the conversations happening in your own head.

It is powerful to witness the generosity, confidence, openness, and integrity of another person. It is a humbling and enriching experience to be on the receiving end of an individual who is genuinely interested in understanding where you are coming from, interested in understanding your experience or your issue, interested in your opinion, and basically interested in creating connection, clarity, new options, or resolution. I have seen a room filled with tension, anxiety, and conflict completely decompress and level out when it is met with this presence and authenticity in action. When someone is not interested in being right but rather in elevating the conversation or interaction to a place of understanding, that is real power—the power of influence. This type of influence leaves a situation changed, people more aware, and the moment remembered.

You can tell how this level of presence and influence from another person affects a room by the number of energized conversations about respect and admiration that bubble up afterward.

If you take away nothing else from this book but the principle of understanding versus being right, it will change many aspects of your life in profoundly amazing ways. This principle has been around for thousands of years and has been taught and written about philosophically, academically, and spiritually.

I've never met anyone who has described wanting to go through life feeling anxious and defensive and missing out on opportunities to connect, thrive, collaborate, innovate, and create. I have met people who want things to be easier, less stressful, more fun—people who want to feel more confident, have more support, and be included in ways that allow them to shine. Awakening to and aligning yourself with an intention of *understanding* is how the shift can occur.

No law or ordinance is mightier than understanding.
(Plato)

Tips for Your Development

○ This exercise helps create the awareness and clarity needed to more easily recognize your own patterns of needing to be right. Spend the next few days observing and listening to the interactions of the people around you. Take note of how much energy is spent on defending, justifying, criticizing, and blaming. After observing and listening, assess how much energy, resources, inspiration, collaboration, innovation, real problem-solving, commitment, and connection is lost as a result. Simultaneously try to notice interactions in which people operate from a position of generosity, understanding, and confidence. What dynamics are fostered there?

○ Identify your three favorite—yes, favorite—ways of being right. Don't judge them, just identify them (If you need a mental nudge, revisit examples in chapter 3). Then make a conscious commitment to specifically watch for these patterns over the next four weeks. When you observe them, use your awareness to shift your intentions and make a different choice in that moment. Working to shift your most common behavioral patterns will stimulate awareness in other areas of your life that are less patterned.

○ Identify a recent situation that left you feeling disconnected and polarized. Circle back and clean up the situation by acknowledging and owning how you contributed to the lack of understanding or disconnect. I'm not suggesting that you return to the situation to accept that you were wrong but that you reclaim an opportunity to understand and connect with the other person or group. This level of honesty and accountability displays profound personal courage and integrity and will build trust and confidence with others. It will also accelerate your own clarity and confidence exponentially.

○ While you are awakening and developing the ability to recognize your blind spots and see dynamics around you with awareness and meaning, having a system of feedback can be a powerful tool to support and promote the awareness. Ask several people you trust to give you feedback when they witness or experience you slipping into patterns of needing to be right, as well as when they experience you developing patterns of trying to understand. This exercise is more powerful once you are aware and can acknowledge your patterns of needing to be right.

4
ABUNDANCE

The single most important decision any
of us will ever make is whether or not
to believe the universe is friendly.

—Albert Einstein

I WAS SITTING with a VP of a Fortune 1000 company, and he told me about a series of events that unfolded during the gas crisis the year before. Things got pretty bad for the organization's employees, as it did for many companies around the United States. The hardest hit was employees with moderate to significant commutes, coupled with tighter personal budgets. The hardship went from painful to unmanageable for many people. The CEO of the company pulled his team together and said, "We have to do something to help our people. We can't just stand by and watch them struggle like this." They explored multiple options, with the CEO getting pushback from his executive team because this idea or that idea would be too hard to implement, or it would negatively affect their margins.

The CEO finally challenged his team by saying that anyone can be resistant, limited, and rigid in his or her thinking and attitude about possibility and the ability to do something transformational. They settled on two interventions. First they allowed employees to buy gas at a discount from the company, and second they allowed division directors to create flex schedules for people to work different shifts to reduce the amount of commuting. The VP went on to say, "I can't do it justice when I tell you the effect this had. We have always had high productivity—people love working here—but the productivity reported by division directors went way up over those months. In addition, our profits were up at the end of our fiscal year. That may have nothing to do with the actions we took, but the bottom line is, I'm a changed man in terms of doing the right thing for the right reason." The CEO wanted no publicity on what they had done, commenting, "I don't do this as a PR stunt or to get more out of people. I do this because it is the right thing to do, and I have been fortunate to have dedication, loyalty, and innovation help me build the enterprise we have today." The VP added that the company has a philosophy and set of values that state, "Prosperity is the by-product when you treat people well and with generosity." The VP said, "It's part of the DNA of our CEO."

The exploration and application of an "abundance" mentality versus a "scarcity" mentality has been applied in many different fields, from economics to management, from personal development to spirituality. The mentality of scarcity is so integrated into our lives that we are frequently unaware of its effects on our attitudes. The system of capitalism, in which we are a part of, is based on a premise of scarcity, otherwise known as opportunity costs. Put another way, I must give something up to get something else; and even though I may not be lacking, I find myself caught in the polarization between wants. Rather than experience it as an abundance of choice, I get lost in the scarcity of fear of losing or not getting something.

The term *mentality* is about mental models, which is used to describe constructs or paradigms that create patterns in the way we think and behave. In other words, do you engage people, scenarios, and ideas around you with an open, curious, and expansive attitude—mentality? Or is it limited, restrictive, and defensive?

Mental models of scarcity and abundance create mentalities within us and, as a result, reciprocal attitudes that have powerful influence over our life experiences. These mentalities form the mental, attitudinal, and relational characteristics in organizational cultures. They determine the outcomes of casual interactions, personal relationships, and important work collaborations. They influence and impact our beliefs about what is and is not possible.

Let's look at the principles of abundance and scarcity down on a personal level and explore how they influence the way we show up in the world. As we go through life, each of us formulates a complex set of beliefs—about ourselves and others, about the world, about what we can expect, about what is right and what is wrong, about everything. These beliefs form over time from a myriad of experiences, both positive and negative, that we have throughout our life. Some beliefs evolve out of personal experience while others come from observations or things we've heard or been taught. These beliefs have a profound influence over our lives, creating a script or mental model—a mentality—that influences and frames the choices we make. This mentality also determines how we choose to engage the world around us.

I like the way author and educator Steven Covey[†] puts this. He suggests that people who are living out a fixed narrative (stuck in their story) in the scarcity mentality see life as having only so much, as if there were only one pie out there; and if someone else gets a big piece of that pie, it would mean less for him or her. Scarcity mentality surges from fear-based beliefs. The fear could come from earlier life experiences or from having seen or heard about another person's experience or outdated stories and perceptions. These fear-based beliefs create fallacies that are projected onto situations either in the moment or in the future. For example, "I'll never get ahead if I collaborate with them— I have to compete," "I could never tell them the truth. They would get mad or reject me," "I can't ask her for help because she never helps anyone."

The scarcity mentality is the zero-sum paradigm of life in which there is only so much money, recognition, time, love and so on to go around—either she gets it, or I get it. People with a scarcity mentality have a difficult time sharing recognition and credit or power and profit, even with people who help in the creation of something. They also

---

[†]   Stephen Covey (b. 1932) wrote the best-selling book *The Seven Habits of Highly Effective People*. He has dedicated his work and teaching to principle-centered leadership.

have a difficult time being genuinely happy for the success of other people. At the core of jealousy, greed and distrust is a profound level of scarcity thinking.

The abundance mentality, on the other hand, flows out of a deep inner sense of personal worth and security. It is the belief that there is plenty of everything for everyone. It results in the sharing of prestige, recognition, profits and decision-making. It opens broader possibilities, options and alternatives and enhances creativity and connection. Abundance or scarcity creates the fertile environment that affects our experiences and outcomes.

Assumptions, those tricky expressions of the imagination attempting to interrupt one's observations and experiences, are actually necessary for navigating the complex, layered and diverse experiences in our daily lives. They offer a critical framework that we use to interpret situations, basically supporting or validating what we think or believe to be true, our perceptions of and projections onto the world around us. Our assumptions are deeply influenced by the beliefs and stories we carry around—in other words, our scarcity and abundance mentalities.

Assumptions can be a wonderful jumping-off point for stimulating deeper insight and more accurate levels of truth in ourselves. Or they can be fueled from the shadows of our fears, creating flawed stories that cause us to react from scarcity-based biases and projections.

When I approach my assumptions from a posture of abundance, I might ask myself, What are you saying to yourself about this scenario? What possibilities in this situation are different from what you were imagining? Is she perhaps different from whom I assumed (the person I heard about and am getting ready to meet)?

I was recently asked to facilitate a quarterly retreat for the board of directors of a public education entity. I was told by several sources that there were difficult and charged relationships inside the group and one person had recently left the board because of the stress of the board environment. In addition, a new person had just been voted onto the board and was described as very contentious. I felt anxiety and scarcity thinking starting to take hold as I created a story about the impending experience. I then pushed the pause button in my head and did what I do when I feel anxiety and scarcity creeping in—I repositioned the story and assumptions, deciding to approach it with the possibility of what might be. This pause allowed me to craft a whole different way of showing up, different from the guy who was guarded and had his script ready. The retreat ended up being an inspirational and highly energized day, with me feeling a huge degree of respect and real affection for the protagonist in the room. What I discovered during the day, which was different from the original story in my head, was that the protagonist was very passionate about the issues facing education and was clearly a strong advocate for students.

Our Lives Are Mediated with Scarcity

Everywhere you turn you are bombarded with messages of scarcity, pessimism and lack, all feeding an almost pathological level of anxiety and fear. These messages are filled with subtle or not-so-subtle narratives of winning and losing, being on the defense against the next enemy, beating out the other guy, or be more like this person and less like yourself. At the core it is not about promoting abundance, prosperity, or mutual trust; it is about promoting the fear-based need to fill the void by competing, attacking, protecting, manipulating, or beating someone else out. Friedrich Nietzsche said, "Pessimism is rampant in cultures on their way out." From my experience his comment also pertains to individuals because negative and scarcity thinking fuel all trips to the bottom.

When you pause for a moment and look with a critical mind and an open heart, you see the palpable and diametric difference between these mentalities of scarcity and abundance. When you buy into scarcity thinking, you have a pessimistic and negative attitude, and your body holds on to exaggerated fear, anxiety, and reactiveness, which shut out the possibility for anything different from what your fear can conjure.

When you are present with abundance thinking, your attitude contains optimism and possibility. You are filled with calm, confidence, and gratitude—or anticipation—about what is possible.

Scarcity Beliefs Fall into Three Broad Assumption Categories

Dr. Len Leritz, a mentor I had early in my career, identified sets of assumptions that form out of our scarcity and abundance beliefs.

Our first scarcity assumption is a fear that there is not enough—not enough resources in the world for us, not enough time, not enough opportunity, not enough other people to help us. At the core we are afraid that *we* are not enough to do what we need to do over time to get the results that we desire. We may be saying to ourselves:

○ I do not have enough time to get it done or do a good job.

- ○ I won't get the opportunity to show what I can do.
- ○ I won't have enough money.
- ○ I better not even try because I am sure I will not be able to do it.

When we fear there is not enough, we assume we have to compete with others for whatever is scarce. This is our second scarcity assumption. We begin perceiving and judging others as greedy and only interested in securing their own advantage. We find ourselves saying things like the following:

- ○ If I don't keep an eye on him, he will take advantage of me.
- ○ They don't care about good service, only their profit.
- ○ I need to grab this before she gets it. She would do the same thing.

Our third scarcity assumption is that we need to plan and strategize if we want to get enough. We need to be more clever and manipulative than others to make sure we get our share. So we find ourselves being deceptive, aggressive, political, and subversive.

Out of these scarcity assumptions, we create fallacies and projections and then engage the world as if they are true. When scarcity responds back from the world around us, that further solidifies our scarcity assumptions. This dynamic is also referred to as the *self-fulfilling prophecy*.

I once watched an unfortunate scenario unfold with an executive of an organization I'd been engaged with for over a year. My first encounter with Ray was in a leadership meeting where I observed him initiate an awkward level of competitive posturing with his colleagues. While debriefing with the CEO after the meeting, I asked him casually about Ray. He said Ray had joined them from the parent company about two years prior. He went on to say that Ray is technically bright and seems ambitious, but he is always concerned things are happening behind his back. He also is the first to go behind others' backs. The CEO also raised concern about Ray's lack of transparency on important issues going on in his division and the level of stress he creates in important projects—such as the important IT launch.

I was a bit surprised later that week when Ray asked to have lunch with me. He launched into a lengthy download about how I should watch out for numerous dynamics within the organization. There were two main themes at the center of his thinking: on one hand, he feared for his job; and on the other, he felt like he was the right successor to the CEO role. Over the following months he continued to behave in a negative manner. He withheld information from the leadership team to control his budget. He took credit for the work of his direct reports. He raised issues to me about the CEO but then told the CEO in meetings he would follow him anywhere (I sat in a bit of shock when I heard that one).

I confidentially set up a one-on-one session with him to see if I couldn't help him get recentered. I decided to hit him straight on with unfiltered honesty and a heavy dose of compassion. The first thing out of my mouth was, "Ray, I am going to speak to you with complete honesty and respect. You are swimming in turbulent waters, my man, and you need a life vest." I then asked, "What is all the scarcity thinking and fear about? Everything out of your mouth is about how you can't trust people, how people don't recognize your contributions, how you are better for this role or that role. Do you understand what is going on here?" He started with a justification that he had to look out for himself and that I did not understand. I said, "Please, tell me what it is I don't understand." He said, "You've not been through what I've been through, so you don't know. I've had to fight for what I have. Things don't come easy." I said,

"You're right. You make a fight out of everything, and you make it so difficult. You can't imagine it being any different." I then asked him if he would like it to be different because it does not have to be such a struggle.

About two months after Ray and I had our intense, unfiltered conversation, I got a call from the CEO, saying he wanted to talk through his pending decision about Ray. He said Ray was becoming a toxic influence in the company, and rather than being an important leadership resource, particularly with important initiatives unfolding, he creates difficulty and stress during a time they need to strengthen confidence and trust throughout the organization. The CEO went on to say, "I've lost all confidence and trust in Ray, and I'm going to ask him to resign." I said, "This might be what it will take for him to wake up."

Abundance Beliefs Also Fall into Three Broad Assumption Categories

Our first abundance assumption stems from a deep belief and trust that something more powerful is at play than what we individually control. Part of that is believing in an interdependence among people, which ultimately becomes a source of abundance. In other words, when I engage the world around me with a belief and attitude of abundance, a natural, reciprocal abundance starts to manifest with others. It is the law of *like attracting like*. This assumption comes from an attitude that there is more than enough people to cooperate with us and love us and that we are more than enough to do what we need to do.

The second abundance assumption is that other people are not greedy. They are just needy like us. They are not trying to beat everyone else out. They are mostly just trying to get their needs met. From this place of abundance we have a strong sense of trust that "I am safe," "You are safe," and "It is safe." We can take risks and explore what is possible, which leads to creating new levels of abundance.

Our third abundance assumption is that our best approach for getting what we need is one of understanding. We get the best results when we are willing to understand reality—the truth in the moment about ourselves and what we need, as well as about others, how they perceive the situation and what they need. We are willing to stay open to the possibilities in our situation.

I was in British Columbia facilitating a four-day collaboration and learning summit with three nongovernmental organizations (NGOs), also known as nonprofits. Although nonprofits frequently share common visions and values in the work they do, they also compete for public funding and donor dollars.

The week unfolded with a great deal of information sharing and talking about best practices and common priorities within the regions where they worked. During the afternoon of the second day, when we were digging deeper into best practices and defining areas for possible change, one of the leaders from the largest agency said he would be happy to share how his organization helps self-directed communities evolve. The rest of the crowd displayed an immediate flurry of surprise and appreciation for the openness and generosity of this agency—that it was willing to share its research and tested experience. Over the next two days the group engaged in a joint learning and planning session that took advantage of individual agency experience to raise the overall knowledge in the group and inform efforts moving forward. They left the session agreeing to explore how they might collaborate on grants to ultimately increase funding for all. This visible level of trust and abundance thinking around how to innovate and build partnership was profoundly inspiring for me.

Father Pius Harding at Mount Angel Seminary shared this story with me:

A wealthy couple was heading off on their honeymoon. It had been arranged for them to visit Mother Teresa at one of her facilities in Calcutta. After they took the tour they commented on how impressed and moved they were by the work being done at the center. The groom wrote out a check for five hundred dollars and handed it to Mother Teresa. She thanked him and told him that it would make a real difference in supporting the center. He replied, "Oh, it's nothing." She gently handed the check back and said, "If it's nothing, then it won't be helpful here." He, without hesitation, immediately made out another check with an additional zero.

Mother Teresa's comment shows us that giving because you have excess does not necessarily come from a place of abundance. Giving something meaningful, something from the heart, accomplishes great things. It was not a question of whether the gift was five hundred dollars or five thousand dollars but whether it came from an attitude of abundance.

Abundant or Naive?

One question that frequently comes up when I talk about scarcity versus abundance is, isn't it naive to assume people are interested in your well-being? Sometimes there is not enough, and people do not care about whether you get your needs met.

I am not suggesting we be naive. To be naive is to be simplistic, unaware, inexperienced, and unrealistic. I am suggesting we automatically set others up to meet our worst or best expectations of them. We use a set of assumptions to frame a situation, and those assumptions create the fertile space for something to unfold and manifest.

I am both amused and dismayed when I hear comments like, "I knew before I even walked into the room that he was going to—." I usually remind the person they pretty much guaranteed the outcome with their predisposed beliefs, assumptions, and attitude of scarcity.

The capacity for abundance thinking requires deep and confident trust. You must trust yourself enough to show up and bring an attitude of abundance and possibility to create something different in each situation. If you need to set a boundary because something questionable is taking place, you can do that and never waiver from your trust and sense of what is possible. I want you to sit with that concept for a moment and imagine what it would be like to be that present and powerful.

The principle of reciprocal cooperation applies to abundance attitudes. The assumption underlying this principle is this: you can get more done and do it easier and better when you cooperate with one another. For example, when you approach me from an attitude (an intention) of generosity and cooperation, you are on more solid ground with yourself. If at any time I begin to step outside the boundary of reciprocal cooperation and treat you in a noncooperative or self-serving manner, then you can draw a boundary with me to get my attention—but not in a way to punish me. You can let me know you are not willing to be taken advantage of by me, yet you would like to cooperate with me whenever I'm willing to pivot back into the circle of collaboration and act in mutually beneficial ways. You never have to leave your attitude (intention) of abundance and trust.

Influence through Connection

Have you ever seen two bodies of water come together? It is chaotic where the different levels connect, and then the water settles at a common level. Interactions between people are like bodies of water coming together. Just like water, people find a common level from which to interact. That moment of coming together offers a profound opportunity to influence how something will play out, basically what *level* you and I will engage. I consciously intend to be an influencing presence in my interactions with others.

After years of business travel, one particular incident illustrates the power of generosity and connection with others. I was flying back to the west coast out of Boston. It was the classic early-evening chaos with hectic and stressed travelers crowded into departure areas. As I got close to my gate, it became clear that my flight was seriously delayed to the point they didn't even know when it would leave—or if it would at all. I took a moment to center myself so as not to fall into the dark side of disappointment and turn the situation into a catastrophe. I stood there for a moment and told myself to let go and not try and control an uncontrollable situation. I then got in line to find out what could be arranged for alternative connections.

While I stood in line, I heard from fellow passengers a lot of blame, accusations, and stories of self-importance or how life was coming apart over this delay. As I got close to the counter, I witnessed some passengers manipulating and strategizing as they tried to negotiate with—and intimidate—the gate agents. It was one of those surreal moments when you are dumbfounded by the unconsciousness of your fellow man and shocked by the lack of basic decent behavior. It was easy to read the body posture, facial expressions, and eye gestures of the agents as they attempted to be present. Most of them looked as if they had left their bodies to escape the wrath being dished out.

As I approached the counter, I thought, *I'm going to be different here*. I said to the agent, "Hi, Kathy. This is a pretty challenging and stressful situation for you. You must feel like you are in a battle zone." She paused and looked at me, and her eyes and shoulders relaxed. She said, "Oh yes. I treat them like a greedy group of thirteen-year-olds." I then asked, "What are we going to do with me?" She said, "Just a moment." Then she smiled, leaned toward me, and quietly said, "I am putting you on a flight through Denver, and it leaves in forty minutes." I felt that moment of excitement that comes from being treated to something special. I said, "Thank you. I am so appreciative." She said, "You're welcome, and thanks for laughing with me."

Where Is the Resistance?

Because many of us struggle with our humanness and perceived shortcomings, we do not default to abundance mode. Our patterns of scarcity stem from an unconscious and reactive place, where finely tuned defenses develop out of the old narratives and fallacies we've told ourselves throughout our lives. The capacity for abundance can be developed, however. We first have to become aware of our patterns with scarcity and then set an intention to reframe our mode of thinking and our beliefs.

The more we question and challenge—not moralize or judge—our scarcity assumptions, the more quickly our attitude and behavior will shift. Transitioning attitudes of scarcity to abundance means we have to be willing to challenge the behaviors or thinking we want to change. For instance, that pattern where you wait for someone to ask you to participate on the project or recognize your ability to add value, you could shift and respectfully offer to assist or show your enthusiasm for the project and your desire to participate. This is a great moment right now to get real with yourself about these patterns. Some will hold on to cynicism to protect themselves from the possibility of failure. Cynicism simply means, it hurts to care. It's the way we buffer ourselves from caring so we don't get let down, and of course, our fears end up being realized. The initial challenge is to recognize the scarcity thinking (cynicism) that blocks our ability to even look at our scarcity mentality. Recognize the resistance and explore what is behind it. What's the story you are holding on to? This approach can help you understand it, decompress it, and start to rewrite the story. Your scarcity stories are outdated, so take a deep cleansing breath and let them go.

Universal Law

A set of laws can be described in scientific terms or in spiritual terms. One of these spiritual or universal laws focuses on "flow." The law of flow holds that the universe does not operate out of scarcity. It never withholds something out of fear that it will not be fruitful. The universe is dynamic and never ceases. It pours forth with an innate force to continually create something more.

Successful organizations and people consciously choose to develop and function from an abundance mentality. If it is not collaboration and win-win, then it will be destruction and lose-lose. This attitude of abundance and full potentiation for all participants is the critical path to the successful organization and successful person of today and tomorrow.

Tips for Your Development

Do this activity as a written exercise:

- Identify your three core scarcity beliefs. Don't judge them. Just name them. These beliefs will feel most familiar. They repeat and show up more frequently than others. Next identify the assumptions that you've developed to keep those beliefs alive and relevant. What is the narrative that supports the belief?
- Can you identify the impact or implications of those beliefs? Can you describe how they have served or not served you?
- Now replace each of your scarcity beliefs with a corresponding abundance belief. Rewrite each belief as an abundance belief. Don't worry about whether you believe it when you write it.
- Based on these new abundance beliefs, what might be the corresponding narrative of success behind each belief? Write it out as you would with an aspiration or vision of what is unfolding.

5

BOUNDARIES

I cannot give you the formula for success,
but I can give you the formula for failure;
which is: Try to please everybody.

—Herbert Swope

I WAS FACILITATING a planning session with a group of business owners and community leaders in a city on the West Coast. They were developing the next phase of a visitors' plan to promote tourism and conventions in their community. Catherine, one of the tourism council members who was convening the meeting, started to get some pretty heated criticism that could have quickly derailed the productivity of the dialogue. After a moment and before I chose to step in, she calmly and confidently said to her antagonist, "I appreciate that this is stressful and time-consuming. Rather than criticize me, you could help by giving me feedback on how I could make this more effective—I would be very open to that."

Her irritated counterpart shifted instantly into an apology and started backtracking and trying to explain himself. She quickly replied, "I appreciate how important this is to everyone, and your participation is critical to a good outcome." You could see people in the group shift as they sat up and slightly leaned in. I noticed the level of respect and confidence in her instantly expanded as she set a boundary of how she wanted to engage and keep the meeting productive and effective. The dialogue and the tone shifted in the group: people became more focused and open and simultaneously more relaxed, which elevated everyone's level of engagement and creativity.

As people were leaving the meeting, it was fascinating and enjoyable to overhear the comments about how the afternoon was more fun than expected.

The topic of boundaries can be both awkward and enlightening because we are all familiar with the opportunities and challenges of creating healthy boundaries in our personal and professional lives. This subject has a way of illuminating patterns of how we live our lives, how we engage and connect with others and how we show up in the world. The types of boundaries we set can tell a rich and revealing story of who we are. They show what we stand for, what we think and believe is important, and what we fear or resist.

I came to a very real and rather painful understanding of the word *boundaries* when I realized they are not simply "dividing lines" but rather how I show up in the world. Early in my career my mentor pointed out that I struggled with weak boundaries. He told me, "If you don't know what you stand for, you will fall for anything, and then you will spend significant amounts of time and energy both defending and trying to find yourself." I knew the relevance of those comments because I felt defensive. The patterns of my weak boundaries were pretty easy to identify because they were a constant source of anxiety and frustration and even a lack of credibility, which was my greatest fear.

I frequently felt the pressure of getting others' approval, the awkwardness of avoiding criticism, and of course, the discomfort of agreeing when I was actually not in agreement. I fundamentally lacked the intentional clarity to know what was important to me, the courage to be honest with others, and the fortitude to have a point of view. I spent significant amounts of energy trying to shift myself back into balance time and time again, and that is an exhausting, frustrating, and demoralizing experience.

"What a flake," I remember saying judgmentally about myself one day when I was reflecting on the patterns that made up a significant part of my life. In that moment of clarity, I was aware of my desire for real connection with others, to be experienced as credible, and to elicit trust and confidence from others. It was sobering to grasp that my weak boundaries were a direct contradiction to what I deeply desired and valued. As I navigated through the disappointment in myself and found some compassion and understanding, I was able to tap into a strong sense of how committed I was to evolve this part of myself. I knew I didn't want to defensively swing to the polar opposite and become tough and bullish, but rather, I wanted to use courage and integrity to begin to operate from my centeredness and confidence. Once I had clarity, commitment and courage—and a healthy dose of humility—there was no turning back on this newfound part of myself.

Implications

The health, quality and vitality of all relationships correlate directly to the quality of the boundaries each person brings into the relationship. Boundaries are an ever-present dynamic filled with challenge, anxiety, opportunity and excitement.

I have met people who wander around in the world with no boundaries. They subject themselves to the demands, pressures, wants and opinions of others to such a degree that they won't claim any personal clarity, definition or desire for themselves. They have difficulty identifying their own wants and needs. They struggle with forming and expressing an opinion, and they struggle with commitments. They walk around feeling confused, powerless, stressed, overwhelmed, and insecure.

On the opposite side of having no boundaries are people whose boundaries are so rigid and inflexible that they are unable to allow anything new or different in their life. They fear that it might challenge their assumptions, ideas, beliefs and projections or shift them out of their well-managed comfort zone. They feel a compelling need to not be out of control and, therefore, resist anything outside of what they know or have experienced before.

Boundaries exist on a continuum, and the aforementioned are the more extreme ends of the spectrum. Our boundaries can move and shift depending on what is occurring in the world around us, as well as inside us. How our boundaries shift ultimately influences how we choose to show up and engage.

The abundance and scarcity mentalities that we explored in chapter 4 provide the active ingredients for how our boundaries manifest. Our attitudes around abundance and scarcity create the framework, characteristics, and dynamics of our boundaries. If we engage our scarcity-based fears and anxieties, we will behave with defensive boundaries that reflect this distorted view. Similarly, when we engage with confidence and clarity from abundance, we'll experience a completely different boundary dynamic.

I want you to become aware of the fears or anxieties that promote the behavior patterns of your boundaries. This level of awareness in the moment allows you to make a choiceful shift with your boundaries. In that moment your boundaries can move from limited and reactive to expansive and responsive because they are coming from a place of awareness, confidence and intention.

I was having dinner with a colleague and his wife at their home. He had just finished having a stern conversation with their six-year-old daughter before she went to bed (I didn't hear the full conversation). As she turned to go up the stairs, she paused, looked at her father, and said without hesitation, "Dad, you're not always right, and I'm not always wrong." The three of us sat there in what I would describe as profound humility. He called to her gently as he walked over to the bottom of the stairs. He sat down on the landing, looked at her, and said, "Yes, that is true—I'm sorry." The next hour of dinner was spent talking about the power of presence and how it gets our attention. Boundaries know no age limits.

Confusion About Boundaries

Boundaries are frequently misunderstood or misrepresented. Many people think boundaries provide defense— the rigid walls we put up to protect ourselves, the reaction we default to when we end up overpowering a situation, or the distractions we create to avoid something that makes us uncomfortable. These behaviors are indeed our defenses. They are those finely tuned protective mechanisms that come out of our unconscious ego, which keep us distracted with the fallacy that we need to be protected.

I affectionately relate to the ego as an entity that runs around with me. It is moderately to severely paranoid and likes to see drama and life-threatening danger around every corner and in every interaction outside its comfort zone.

The best counsel I've heard on dealing with the ego is this: It doesn't need to be argued with. It doesn't need to be overpowered. It just needs some firm, nonthreatening direction. Basically, sit down and shut up. You're going to be fine.

Boundaries give you clarity about what is important and where your energy and commitment could or should be focused. Boundaries display your values and conviction and engage your courage and focus.

Boundaries can be felt in your body before they show up externally because they activate creative tension, which points out an opportunity to shift and then engage with clarity and intention. This could signal an opportunity to be courageous and step out of your comfort zone of acting confused or avoiding something. It might make you aware of when you need to practice restraint—those moments when you need to pause, listen more, and be present rather than talk, lecture, control, or assert yourself.

In other words, moments of clarity and intention may challenge you to expand your boundaries and soften your rigidity so you can shift into exploration and generosity with a person or situation. Likewise, you may need to mobilize boundaries of personal power to assert yourself and step forward when something has confronted your values, sense of well-being, or what you believe to be right in the moment.

Understanding how your boundaries feel in your body when they get awakened gives you a sense of clarity, calm, confidence, and presence, which in turn helps you know when and how to respond. Your boundaries make it easy for people to know who you are and what you stand for. They tell a story that extends far beyond just what you do.

Boundaries are diametric to defenses. They feel different in your body and different to the world around you. Your defense system is an amazing and finely tuned response that can mobilize you to avoid or protect yourself in the face of harm or threat. However, most of the situations you face in life neither pose threat nor harm to you, but it sure can feel that way when your defenses are triggered.

When you operate out of your defenses, your feelings should be obvious: reactive, hot, insecure, aggressive, fearful, and judgmental. Likewise, there should be no confusion about your feelings when you operate from your boundaries: confident, calm, energetic, centered, open, respectful. It's the place where your heart and head are connected. Your boundaries center you in a sense of clarity without necessarily needing answers. Confidence and generosity make it easier for you to be open, inviting and energized. This type of energy, openness and presence also influence how others around you will show up and engage. This centered and intentional place is the place of being versus doing—that place below the waterline, where our authentic power lives.

A nonprofit agency asked me to be on its board. A couple of months prior to this request, I decided to take a break from board activity because I had just completed a five-year board position. When this organization asked me to join the board, however, I asked them why they wanted me on the board. I wanted to be intentional in my decision and honor my need to take a break. They said they would like to do some strategic visioning work with me about the future of the agency. I told them I would be happy to work with them, and I didn't think I needed to be on the board to be a contributor. They agreed.

This simple example shows how my boundaries created clarity around my priorities and to what I could commit. And this clarity enabled me to continue to contribute—something that's important to me.

Boundaries Build Capacity

The boundaries that we are talking about here are distinct and compelling because they are not dogmatic, rigid, or threatening. They are adaptive because they respond to the context of a situation, responsive because they come out of intention, understandable because they come out of clarity, safe and respectful because they come out of courage and integrity. These boundaries take less time and energy and consume fewer resources than putting up defenses—and in fact, they are energizing.

As you intentionally become more connected to your own values and evolve your higher-level boundaries, you will see a profound shift in how the world around you responds and opens up. Developing the awareness to know how your higher-level boundaries feel inside you, sound to others, and look in your behavior will increase your ability to build capacity and adaptiveness in them.

You actually negotiate boundaries all day long. You do this when you encounter other drivers on the road, when you decide what is a priority or a distraction, what is really important in your interaction with another person or group, how you will choose to handle or manage a difficult situation, and when it makes sense to extend yourself with generosity and understanding. When you operate from a conscious, responsive and open place, your boundaries manifest as clear, intentional and profoundly influential.

I got a call from Jason, a physician in his late twenties and a year out of his medical residency program. He had been in a workshop with me six months prior to calling and was anxious to talk about a significant ("life-changing," as he described it) conversation he had with his parents the day before. He proceeded to tell me he had mustered the courage to stand in his truth and share the secret he'd been keeping from his parents—that he is gay. He described what he felt before the conversation and the details of what unfolded during the conversation. He said he felt clear and confident and had a huge level of self-respect when he made the decision to talk with them.

When Jason told his parents, they just looked at him and then started to debate the reality of what he was telling them. He said they immediately started throwing in obstacles and denial—not being aggressive or rude exactly but being very resistant and defensive. He stopped the conversation after a moment and said, "I understand you are feeling some level of shock, much like I did when I came to accept the truth for myself. I need you to understand that I am open to helping you understand and explore what this all means, and I am willing to talk about it in any way that will help you process and come to terms. I need you also to know I will not defend myself to you or feel wrong or be treated with disrespect."

He said his parents then stopped talking, and their faces shifted. I asked him what he thought was happening for them in the moment. He said, "They were no longer self-absorbed, and they were able to see me as their son versus something to react to."

Jason said this experience opened something profound in him: the ability to recognize and stand confidently and calmly in his own truth. He believes he would develop into a more confident and compassionate physician as he develops this level of awareness and centeredness in himself.

"It was not prearranged," said Rosa Parks. "It just happened that the driver made a demand, and I didn't feel like obeying his demand. I was quite tired after spending a full day working."

In 1955, at the age of forty-two, Rosa Parks[‡] came to the moment of clarity that was less about her rationale than it

---

[‡]   Rosa Parks (1913–2005) was an African American civil-rights activist. She was notable for her refusal to give up her seat on a bus for a white passenger. The US Congress called

was about her values, her sense of self-respect, and where she would draw the boundaries of decency and dignity. Her boundaries in that moment were called civil disobedience, and they came from a woman with no formal power or social standing. Yet her boundaries of clarity, courage, confidence, and self-esteem contributed to the influence that changed a nation.

She is quoted as saying, "I have learned over the years that when one's mind is made up, this diminishes fear, knowing what must be done does away with fear."

We don't need to promote or debate our boundaries or really even talk about them in most situations—that is what we do when we need to defend something or drive a point. Boundaries are an unspoken language much like cultural language. They are integrated into how we show up and engage with others and simply become part of the fabric and texture of how others experience us.

Boundaries are almost more about what isn't said than what is said. They come from our values and tell a nar-

---

her the first lady of civil rights and the mother of the freedom movement.

rative about who we are and what we are made of. One's values might be of honesty, integrity, fearlessness and generosity. We don't have to describe this to people or warn them. When we simply engage and behave from our values, our boundaries emerge automatically. I like to say people always know how to treat you and connect with you by how you engage with them and how you live your principles and values. You show your boundaries by simply being your true self.

Tips for Your Development

- Name the values you want to show up with in the world. How are these articulated through your behavior? And do these come across in the way others experience you? I'm not talking about a laundry list of values that you think you should have or the ones posted in the coffee room of your company. These are a set of values you really want fully integrated into your personality and actions—how you show up. They are the ones that are nonnegotiable.
- Write or relate a simple narrative about how you would like others to refer to you after you leave a room. How would they describe their experience with you?

○ How do your current boundaries help create the perception you described in the narrative?

○ Ask three or more people whom you know and trust to be honest with you (not tell you what they think you want to hear). How would they describe your current boundaries? What kind of experience do you create with others, personally and professionally?

6

DEFINING NEEDS

TWO EMPLOYEES APPROACHED me on different days with the same solution to their issues: they needed a raise. Eric came to my office late in the afternoon to talk about something he had been feeling a lot of resentment about. After taking a long centering breath, he told me he needed a raise. I asked what a raise would give him (in other words, what was his need?). He said he didn't feel respected in the company and that it would make him feel more respected. I asked him to tell me how this respect was not happening. With good clarity he talked about how he felt invisible with his work. He never got feedback or recognition and basically felt like he wasn't important in the department. He believed if he were to receive a raise, that would mean he was important and recognized. (Sidenote with some context: Eric was in one of the highest-paid disciplines in the company, and the company was in one of the highest-paying industries. So by most standards, he was in the top tier of paid professionals.)

As we talked about what he was experiencing professionally, he shifted off the pay raise and talked about what he needed personally to feel rewarded and inspired. A couple of solutions came out of the discussion. First he was going to approach his director and start an informal discussion about the direction of the department and what his director would like to see from him. Second I was going to do some assessment of what others in the department were experiencing in terms of morale and motivation.

Several weeks after I met with Eric, another employee, Shelly—from a different discipline and division—came to my office. With a tenor of confidence and some degree of lightheartedness, she told me how she had to work two jobs to make ends meet, which she described as relatively modest. She shared how much she loved working here and how much she enjoyed the work she was doing. She felt like she made a real contribution to the level of quality in her department. However, she needed to get into a better salary situation. Shelly didn't want to leave the company before exploring what was possible. Her needs were to be financially stable and reduce her stress about making ends meet. I told Shelly to give me two days to get back to her. Two solutions came out of the follow-up. Shelly got an immediate raise, and we changed the salary ranges in her department as well.

We did a quick review of the salary categories for her discipline and found we were below the market range. Eric's and Shelly's needs were different, yet they both had the same solution—more money. I was moved by each of their stories but felt resistant to Eric's solution because it didn't address his true need. Shelly was clear about her needs, and she trusted that simply articulating them would create movement in the necessary direction.

Many people have become blindly conditioned to a subtle yet common dynamic related to how we engage and work in most aspects of our lives. It is insidious because most people are unaware of its implications in the moment but are left feeling the impact and void after the fact. I'm talking about the confusion or disconnect between *needs* and *solutions*. In fact, many people scratch their heads in confusion when they try and differentiate the two.

Needs and solutions have been so conveniently lumped together as the same that creating context and clarity around them is a real challenge. We have become so disconnected from recognizing and identifying our own true needs that we focus on solutions first, and then these get confused with needs. Needs are the most basic motivator behind all human behavior. They inform our decisions and actions in most everything we do.

Cost and Impact

Focusing on misappropriated and premature solutions is a common dynamic inside companies, and when these solutions fail, significant loss can result. Adding insult to injury, company leadership will frequently start throwing more ill-conceived solutions at a problem only to dig the loss hole deeper.

A significant amount of the work I've done in facilitation, strategy and negotiations has been with individuals and leadership teams that have become polarized over solutions instead of working to understand the needs and issues driving the solutions. This dynamic creates strained relationships, eroded trust, loss of credibility, confusion, lost productivity and missed opportunities.

We also display the same patterns in our personal lives, becoming polarized over what to do, when to do it, and how to do it instead of developing clarity and understanding of the actual need. We get defensive, and relationships become pitted and polarized as a result of this dynamic. Our ability to listen, learn, explore and collaborate deteriorates when we are stuck on solutions. Needed conversations don't take place, new possibilities are missed, and confidence in one another is weakened—all of which lead to an erosion of trust. And it's trust that takes intensive time to rebuild.

Getting clear about needs impacts the way we engage, work, and collaborate with others and how we make decisions on our own and together. Lack of clarity can negatively impact us when the solutions we choose don't meet our needs.

A Bit More Clarity

Our tendency to confuse needs with solutions keeps us from really understanding and acknowledging what they are—the real motivators behind people's behavior. *Needs* do not invoke reactions. They are "neither" good nor bad, moral nor ethical issues—they just are. We all have them, and they are pretty much the same for each of us: for things to make sense and have meaning, to be understood and valued, to feel respected and treated fairly, to be able to make a contribution and add value—just some examples. And we experience different needs at different times.

Solutions, however, do cause reactions—they can be good or bad solutions, smart or foolish, supported or resisted.

When we can recognize a reaction or resistance and change focus from solutions to needs, we then gain clarity, context and insight. Having this clarity brings confidence and credibility to the solutions we present and to which we agree.

We have an amazing, fast-paced capacity for problem-solving that equips us to get things done, navigate issues with perceived efficiency, and get what we want without expending too much time on stuff we don't value. The speed of our thinking and processing, although an incredible asset, can disconnect us from taking time to differentiate between a solution and a need. Why is it so important to make this differentiation? A solution does not exist without a need. One forms the viability of the other. Getting clear and grounded of the need driving the solution is critical.

We often think that our solutions are needs. We try to convince ourselves that we are brilliant for taking care of our needs so quickly, but this fast-paced thinking is frequently reactive, blind, and cloaked to appear brilliant and savvy. Reactive thinking can be fueled by impatience, anxiety, fear, scarcity, or arrogance. Upon closer examination, it frequently lacks the clarity, context, confidence and understanding from which real brilliance emanates.

Here are relatively straightforward definitions of the words *need* and *solution*: A need is a "condition, cause or situation requiring relief or change." A solution is a "fix or approach or work-around (one of potentially several) to address the condition or cause." Needs are when the *why* question is answered; solutions are the *what* answer. Getting clear about the why creates clarity about the what. The need is the value proposition. The solution is how we will get there and what we will do, but it's not the why.

Solutions without clearly aligned needs frequently invite opposing positions. When we push what we think is our well-crafted, thoughtful, and creative solution, we frequently challenge others to an arm-wrestling and power-playing match to see who has the best solution. We then falsely try to convince ourselves that our solution makes sense. We need this or that—we want it—so it's obvious that ours is the "right" solution.

But put yourself on the receiving end of what I just described—when someone else presents a solution. You know what I'm talking about. Someone comes at you with a solution: Here's how it should be. This is what we should do, or this is what you should do. You become resistant, defensive, or argumentative—or maybe you cave in to appease the other person, going along with the solution to avoid a fight but walking away uncommitted.

Here are some simple, pragmatic examples to help you further understand and integrate the difference between needs and solutions:

Solutions	Needs
You need to be home by 7:00 p.m.	I want to spend more quality time with you.
Let's go to Palm Springs.	I want to spend time in a sunny, warm place around a pool.
Report on my desk by 5:00 p.m. today.	I need to review the report before meeting the client next Tuesday.
Can you reduce this bid by 20 percent?	I need to understand the costs in this bid.
Let's go out to eat tonight.	I need a break from cooking.
Let's leave the house at 5:00 a.m.	It's spring break. The airport may be busy. I don't want to be late.
I'd rather invite someone else.	I'm concerned your brother will start arguing with his wife again.
We need to cut the costs by 10 percent.	This division has higher costs. Let's find out what is driving them.

Let's send out more e-mails.	Our satellite office feels disconnected from us and wants more inclusion.

I made the comment at the beginning of this chapter that the "disconnect" between needs and solutions is commonplace and insidious. It's commonplace because it is the modus operandi for political leadership, corporate culture and personal relationships. It is the way we address our issues, small and major, in all arenas. It's insidious because we blindly think this is the best way to get things done. We think it's a sign of strong leadership, a reflection of our intellectual prowess. We think it's efficient. It isn't until we have to deal with the impact of this approach that we might get a sense of what's actually unfolding. At that point it takes courage, clarity, and integrity to step back, regroup and recalibrate to clean up the situation and realign in a direction that can get us what we most desire: great outcomes, with others fully engaged and committed.

A Shift in Leadership

Many insightful leaders are beginning to recognize these ineffective patterns. They have seen the strategic implications of putting into place disconnected and ill-conceived solutions that don't address real needs. As a result, many now engage in a more critically explorative process called strategic clarity, which differs from the traditional strategic planning process where the corner offices go off and decide what solutions to implement.

The strategic clarity process is about asking the why questions, getting clear about the value proposition that solutions need to be able to deliver on. To be clear that the needs are really being addressed, this clarity process actually involves people from disciplines and divisions that are ultimately responsible for delivering the outcomes versus managers who oversee the business from a spreadsheet or analytical report. This shift in approach increases the insight that goes into determining solutions. In other words, leadership is truly vetting and understanding the needs that inform the decision-making process—the creation of solutions. The solutions become critical factors that both inform and drive business, engage and level up the commitment of the workforce, and keep the organization aligned with its valued consumer.

Solutions are always in service to needs. In other words, a solution is a by-product of a need. Many of us get sidetracked because we operate from assumptions or projections about what our needs are, but rarely do we get clear enough to really understand them.

How many times have you heard the following after a solution or approach failed? "Well, I assumed this. I assumed that. I assumed that he/she/they were going to—."

Leadership teams across many companies are hearing these kinds of responses to ill-conceived solutions. The feedback falls into two significant categories:

- Employees do not feel like leadership understands who they are, what they do and how the business really works. Leadership seems to make all the decisions from a spreadsheet or while locked away in a corner office.
- Consumers do not feel like a company understands who they are and what they really want. They feel like a statistic or a commodity.

When leadership is so disconnected from critical stakeholders such as employees and customers, it creates missed opportunities, wasted resources and eroded confidence and commitment.

Perhaps Parents Can Relate

Jack was in a negotiation seminar I was teaching. During one of the group exercises, he said, "Maybe you can help me with a situation I've gotten into with my daughter." The group burst out laughing. He smirked. "It sounds funny, but it has become a head-banging-against-the-wall experience." He related that he and his daughter were at a stand-off over curfew. It was becoming intense and creating a lot of discord. He felt she didn't understand or respect why he wanted her home at 10:00 p.m., and she didn't feel like he understood or respected what she wanted. The issue was now becoming about respect.

I asked him if they had talked about what they each needed rather than solely focusing on their individual solutions—he wanted her home at 10:00 p.m., and she wanted to stay out until 11:00 p.m. He looked at me a bit surprised and said, "What do you mean?"

"Glad you asked," I replied. "What do you think your daughter really needs?"

"Um, not sure," he said.

"Step back. Get out of your head and your assumptions and open your awareness," I said. "What do you think she really needs that she feels like you don't get?"

He paused then replied, "I suppose she wants me to trust her. I imagine she wants some independence, probably to feel like she has more freedom."

I smiled and said, "I think you nailed it. At the core of this issue are your needs. The two of you need to talk about what you each need and want to be doing at 10:00 p.m." The 10:00 p.m. mark was the flash point. "I'm hearing that you need to not be awake and worrying about her. You need to know she's okay. You need to know that she is not engaged in anything unsafe or illegal. In short, you need to know that you can trust her, and you want a relationship of mutual respect."

He smiled and said, "Wow, she isn't going to recognize her dad tonight when we talk."

Clearly Identified Needs

A solution that is not the by-product of clearly articulated needs will lack credibility and clarity, and it will usually be met with some level of resistance. In other words, if you don't understand what the needs are, the solution is most likely going to flop. A solution by itself is like giving an answer without knowing the question—it's confusing. When people get confused, they most frequently get defensive and resistant. Pushing solutions without context and clarity of needs and some level of buy-in from everyone involved just pulls people into confusion and defensiveness. I like to remind people that the solution itself isn't going anywhere, so they can calm down and get clear about the needs that drive the solution. It's important to put your energy into creating some fertile turf for the solution to develop. A premature solution is like anything premature— it struggles to live.

People have a litany of reasons for focusing on solutions rather than needs:

- I've spent too much time figuring out the problem and the solution, and I don't have the time or patience to explain it to you.
- I don't want to hear what you need because it might sidetrack what I need.
- To be honest, I don't care what you need. I want my solution.
- My head is running too fast to think about needs other than the ones I can identify.
- If I don't push my solution, I may walk out of here losing.

- You've started to push your solution, so I need to push mine.
- If I come up with the solution, it will make me look smart, important and powerful.
- If my solution doesn't get through, we won't get the budget.
- This client just doesn't get it, so we need to be firm on our solution.
- It's the way it works. You have to be competitive and push your solution through.
- You can't argue. Look where my solutions have gotten me.
- We went with your solution last time.
- We are the experts, so we know more than you.
- I'm the boss, so I know more than you. It's going to be my solution.
- I need to push my solution so I don't appear weak.
- You're the vendor/consultant, and I'm the client, so it should be my solution.
- I'm the parent, and you're the kid, so it's my solution.

Influence Lives Around the Need

In the 1940s Abraham Maslow[§] shifted our understanding of what it means to be human to a more profound reality of what makes us exemplary and motivates our behavior—our needs. He opened up a vast field of study that has given us insight and a framework for understanding why we behave the way we do, which is the deep desire and drive to have our needs met. His research and work helped us better understand human motivators, the basis of our needs. This has helped us become more successful in orchestrating human systems—relationships, organizations, communities and marketplaces.

The ability to influence and find good solutions comes from a willingness and ability to get clarity of needs. The time spent exploring and understanding needs, motivators and underlying objectives creates space for the best possible solution or approach. Confident, centered indi-

---

[§] Abraham Maslow (1908–1970) was an American psychologist considered to be the founder of humanistic psychology. Humanistic psychologists believe every person has a strong desire to realize his or her full potential, to reach a level of self-actualization. Maslow developed a hierarchy of human needs as a path for achieving full potential.

viduals will ask many clarifying questions. They will work toward "uncompromising" clarity. They use their confidence barometer to make sure they are grounded in clarity, not assumptions.

A barometer is a powerful instrument; it measures shifts in atmospheric pressure. This data enables travelers to pack prudently and mariners to set an appropriate course. A confidence barometer is a hypothetical concept that can help explain the power of understanding your inner world, as well as your interactions with others.

Our confidence barometer lets us know how confident we are in any given situation—for example, in understanding needs, issues, motivators and even desires—before we promote a solution or head in a specific direction on an issue. When we are confident, we have a greater level of clarity, which in turn creates space for the solution to develop and thrive. As a result, we don't have to spend time and energy forcing solutions or cleaning up misaligned and misappropriated solutions.

Getting clear about needs impacts how people feel about the way we engage, work, collaborate and make decisions. Getting clear about needs can also have a significant impact on us when premature solutions don't meet our needs. Take a current situation you're involved in and observe the conversation (even if the conversation is just with yourself) when it is focused on needs versus solutions.

Getting Centered in the Conversation

Your ability to stay engaged in inquiry and dialogue until you get clarity on what is needed will give you confidence and momentum for how to proceed. The willingness to keep asking questions provides insight and builds rapport, which ultimately develops into credibility and trust.

People love to lean on the things they trust. When people feel their needs are being recognized, respected, and validated, they relax and move to higher levels of trust. Solutions often fall onto the table in front of you with little effort when this kind of clarity, connection and trust is created. This is an ideal environment for influencing real movement of important issues.

Consider taking the following points of view during your next conversation:

- I need to create clarity.
- I need to instill confidence.
- I need to establish a relationship before I do anything.
- I need to understand what this resistance or stalemate is about.

○ I need to build trust to get the right kind of commitment for the solution.

Several years ago I was in a senior-leadership meeting where we were in an overly energized conversation—more like a polarized debate—about whether to close an international office that was having significant issues. The business performed poorly. The office was plagued with high turnover, and our public relations in the local market had eroded to a shamefully low level. I genuinely liked and respected the people in the room. They had solid integrity, trusted one another, and were pretty insightful—most of the time.

As the debate and thrash continued, I kept quiet and gently backed away (internally) from the chaos so I could center my thinking and observe what was unfolding in the room. One, I knew closing the office would be a huge mistake. Two, yes, the issues were significant, and the office had not been managed well. In addition, the organization had been less than judicious in its choice of leadership for that office. Plus, I recognized a pattern here that I had seen elsewhere in the company. When issues become significant, people love to blame the outside world rather than become accountable as a leadership team.

I continued to sit and observe, staying present but quiet. After about forty minutes of thrashing solutions around— none of which were the product of any insight or agreement of real need—the CEO, clearly seeing the need to get some traction, turned to my palpable quietness and observant demeanor and asked me, "What do you think we should do?"

I paused. Instead of giving him an answer, I started to ask questions about what it was we needed. "Do you want to be in this marketplace?"

"Yes."

"To accomplish globally what you desire, do you need to be in this marketplace?"

"Yes."

"Do you think you've made prudent decisions in managing this office as part of the global network?"

"Probably not."

The group was now tuned in and clearly waiting for my next comment. I continued, "I would agree with your assessment that the place is a mess, and it needs immediate attention just to stop the hemorrhaging." I went on to say, "Make no mistake about one thing. If you close this office, you will never open an office there again. The market won't let you back in, the press won't let you back in, and you won't have the emotional fortitude to really go for it again. You will be so jaded by this incident. So the real question is, How committed are you to clean it up and turn it around?"

The office stayed open, and within eighteen months, it became one of the better-performing offices internationally.

What was going on with me in that moment when I pulled back and got quiet? I knew I had no formal authority to direct a solution, no matter how insightful I thought it might be. It was also apparent that someone would probably power his or her way to a decision, and then the leadership team would deal with the fallout from that decision. I understood that I needed to get the relevant questions on the table. I needed to help move the group away from debating the solution and on to what it was they really needed—a successful global network, a high-performing office—and the issues resolved.

The power of asking questions is that it allows brilliance and creativity to surface. The real power is in the willingness to pause, observe and be with the question as opposed to pushing for a solution. Voltaire said, "Judge a man by his questions rather than by his answers." Developing clarity, context and connection of needs helps elevate influence more than being the person who drives a solution. This is where influence below the waterline lives—the place of being, before doing.

Stay focused on the question until you feel the "aha moment," also known as, "Oh, I get it."

Get Others off Their Solutions

Let's look at this topic from a slightly different angle. How do you shift others off the solution when it's being pushed at you? This dynamic happens in all aspects of our lives and frequently comes from people in perceived positions of power—parents, bosses, clients—just to mention a few. Our intention remains the same: to build and maintain trust, confidence, and clarity and to find the best solution by getting clear on our needs.

At times we think we have no power. I will keep gently reminding you: power comes from your ability to influence, not from your position. When you notice that a solution is being presented, or perhaps even pushed, you have an opportunity to shift in the moment from resistance or debate into curiosity and exploration. This moment allows you to find out what led to the solution, what thinking was behind it. Ask to be brought up to speed on what the other person or group went through to arrive at the solution. You might ask, "Context would be really helpful here. Would you share what you went through to get to this solution? I hear the what, can you share the why?"

Staying in the question space decompresses the need for others to keep driving a solution. It shifts the rapport and opens up the conversation. In this new space of rapport and dialogue, the possibilities start to expand.

The division director with a client company shared a wonderful example with me of her personal epiphany around this pattern of pushing solutions. She and her son Jared were working on a significant project at home, which was taking weeks to complete. Out of frustration and some impressive confidence, Jared approached his mother and told her he was feeling like he couldn't be successful on the project. He felt stressed, anxious and criticized. In addition, he was beginning to feel stupid—like he just couldn't get it. He told her, "I'm not stupid, and I want to do this right, but you just keep telling me what to do, and you never tell me what you are thinking or why. I feel like I am trying to read your mind to understand what you really want, but you only talk to me when you're feeling impatient or you're in a hurry. I assume you want me to do a good job with this project, so you need to spend time helping me understand what you're thinking instead of making me read your mind."

She paused and then said, "Oh no, is that what I'm doing? I'm so sorry." She told me that although she was sorry she had been doing this to her son, something even more significant shook loose in her, like she suddenly could see an old pattern. She asked her son, "Jared, will you tell me more about how I do this?"

She sat with her son's comments all weekend because they exposed a pattern she had heard through her division at work. She said, "I've heard people making not-so-subtle comments that I do this with staff and direct reports. I throw solutions and direction around with no context or thinking behind it. I've been brushing it off as people complaining. How could I be so blind?"

A Bit of Rewiring

The ability to align a conversation around clarification of needs does not come naturally for many people. We easily fall into impatience or a sense of urgency and a desire to implement—driven frequently by a distorted sense that we need to come to solutions more quickly. This causes us to push the process or overmediate the conversation with a checklist of action items. Ultimately we come off as patronizing or heavy-handed. In many situations we simply need to focus and follow a framework for getting real clarity and understanding of needs. Then we can move forward successfully to a solution that is a by-product of clarity and do it in a timely manner.

Be aware that tension can surface when you play with this principle. Don't worry as it is healthy, creative tension. When we move people off their solutions and reengage them in discussion on clarity of needs, resistance can be triggered when they feel disconnected from their original fixed position or solution. It's the distorted fear of losing or being out of control.

Just keep exploring with respectful and confident questions to create clarity, and you will help them decompress and move into alignment with you.

The real power in recalibrating your thinking comes from the intentional awareness of what you are trying to accomplish. That level of awareness only happens when you allow your head and heart to have a conversation. Having this connection within yourself gives you the capacity for real insight and the ability to track multiple levels of conversation and interaction with others. This head-heart connection also allows you to shift your thinking in real time. Your real power comes from your ability to make a conscious choice, the kind of choice where you are clear about your intentions. When you are able to shift from that unconscious, reactive place to the space of being present and aware, you then have the ability to connect and really understand needs. This level of influence enables you to create context and meaning, as well as mobilize commitment and movement for agreed-on solutions and direction.

Tips for Your Development

This concept works well as a written exercise when you are first getting your head around it. Think of a current or recent situation. Make a list of the needs (even if you have to assume what they are) for both parties and then look at the solution currently on the table. Does it really serve the needs? Or is there a better solution based on the clarity you identified in the needs?

For a month identify the needs of any solution that you are applying to a situation, even if it seems simplistic. This practice will help you rewire your circuits to start recognizing the difference between needs and solutions. Being able to do it in simple, less-stressful situations will give you the gravitas to start doing it in more intense and important situations. Basically you are going to be mobilizing your critical-thinking skills.

Get clear about your intentions. When you are trying to understand needs, think and feel in terms of what you truly desire. Make it easy on yourself. Always start out with a question. A question (instead of a comment or statement) alters the dynamic between people. It opens others up and stimulates their curiosity. It expands their capacity to think and relate. Starting out with a question will also center your own thinking and ability to relate. You will feel smarter, and you will make others feel smarter. You will be creating a space for dialogue.

TRANSPARENCY

There are no secrets better kept than the
secrets that everybody guesses.

—George Bernard Shaw

I WAS ATTENDING the annual leadership conference held by one of my clients, an event where the company brings in its top leadership from around the globe. The room was filled with about two hundred people. Later in the morning session, Kevin, the senior VP of three divisions, held a Q and A with the group. Someone from the audience asked about the company's sustainability efforts and preliminary initiatives. This person wanted to better understand how important sustainability really was for the company—whether it was just talk and window dressing or if there was a road map actually directing the efforts.

Kevin spent some time touching on the topic and then paused for a moment. It was one of those moments that get your attention and make you just a bit uncomfortable because it extends about a half second longer than you are conditioned for. He proceeded with, "As I was just now talking about our initiatives around sustainability, what was really weighing on me is an issue that challenges my confidence and sense of integrity even more. As I stand here right now, I'm telling myself to be confident and trust myself to raise the issue here today." He cleared his throat and continued, "Some of our production contracts internationally, like those of many American industries, have been benefiting us with better margins because of substandard employment conditions for many of the people who work there. As I stand here with you today, I know we have to change this. I know that it will create significant work on many people's part. I don't have the answers, and neither does the rest of the leadership team." As he looked over at a team of his peers, he concluded, "We've not started to tackle this issue and have not really had this serious discussion yet, so I am starting the discussion here and now with all of you."

People were buzzing about Kevin's openness and comments all throughout the wine reception after the meeting. One of the women in the group I was with said she, along with several others, grabbed Kevin and told him how much they valued what he did and what it represented for them as leaders. She said he replied by telling them he had been asking himself what kind of leader he really was. Kevin went on to say that he was going to be courageous and not veer from what he knew was right. He said, "I was courageous earlier in my life and was willing to stand up for what I knew was right. Why am I veering from that now?"

For some the term *transparency* has a radical connotation. In recent years people became outraged as they began to realize they had been nothing more than a disposable commodity to the hubristic leadership of many institutions. The fallout from years of corporate and political corruption created a backlash from the public, demanding stronger accountability and oversight. This demand quickly developed into bureaucratic processes aimed at directing new levels of corporate and governmental transparency and accountability. These bureaucratic protocols, although driven at some level by a cultural shift, pale in comparison with the explosion of information and transparency now available through the global Web.

With its accessibility, fluidity, and boundless transparency, the Web has transformed the power of information and connectivity, resulting in an empowered global society. The Web, along with the expansion of the media, has shifted the social physics of information. What was once a secret can now be part of the next exposé on headline news or commentary through any number of social-networking venues.

It's humorous to think that much of anything can be kept a secret today. The new levels of accountability we see in corporate and government sectors are driven less by regulation and more by the power of information, forcing transparency—and the anxiety that no one can hide.

Aspects of this transformational shift also have exposed the shadowy side of transparency, which at times appears as a boundaryless wasteland of sensationalism, where voyeuristic vignettes and deceptive tidbits of information are promoted with little regard for the impact. This sensationalism reveals the interrelatedness of information and the seamlessness of connectivity, but its focus on exposure is quite different from transparency.

Although technology and media are platforms for connecting and engaging communities, these tools can't truly capture the power of authentic transparency.

At the core, transparency enables us to shift the way we engage with others. With transparency, we make a conscious choice to shed the facades, attitudes, distortions, and defenses that take inordinate amounts of energy to maintain. These defenses promote nothing of value but rather feed a distorted sense of protection and power. Transparency allows us to feel confident and clear about who we are and what we stand for. It allows us to operate from a place of authenticity and integrity. We are no longer held hostage by the fear of others seeing into our true being. As the fear of transparency dissipates, we see more choice and opportunity opening up to us. This space of authentic transparency has been described as the *zone*, similar to what athletes experience, which feels powerful and serene—an absence of anxiety or stress and the ability to be present in the moment.

Discussions on transparency frequently turn into debates about the divergent extremes, from the absence of transparency—when power lies in secrecy—justified deception, and convenient manipulation to people with no boundaries at all who become objects of exploitation. To further confuse the discussion, "truth telling" is often injected into the discussion as "You are transparent when you are telling the truth" or "You aren't telling the truth if you're not transparent."

The real meaning and power of transparency gets lost in this debate, and the concept can be used as a manipulative tool when viewed through rules and literal interpretation.

Real transparency offers a powerful principle that can guide our intentions and choices—how we choose to show up in the world at any given time. Real transparency is not a media event or public-relations strategy. It's simply a way of being, which at its core is confident, thoughtful, and anchored in integrity. People in the presence of this kind of transparency experience it differently than they do other forms of controlled, mediated and manipulated "transparency." Authentic transparency profoundly influences the world around it because we shift and change when we are in the presence of this level of clarity, integrity, humanity, and confidence. It motivates and inspires us. It elicits confidence and trust and causes us to gravitate closer to it because we experience it. In the midst of that experience, we are pulled into our own humanity—it becomes a mirror for us.

Transparency, as used in a social context, generally implies openness, communication and accountability. You can see through a transparent object. You can easily understand a transparent situation, which puts you at ease and creates connection with others. When we can connect with people, understand them, make sense of them, feel their experience and see congruently in their story, we create connection and congruity in ourselves. It stimulates our own capacity for transparency.

Personal Insight

This idea of "seeing through" provided a real breakthrough in my understanding of transparency as a principle or personal characteristic rather than a behavior. When we see into someone, it creates clarity and insight about him/her, which stimulates confidence and increased trust—the qualities that move us to more authentic forms of reciprocal engagement. We are more likely to invest time and energy with people when we understand them and can connect with them. They have meaning.

What does it feel like when someone can see into me? The first time I asked myself this question, the idea felt disconcerting and made me feel out of control and too vulnerable. I could be taken advantage of. When I acknowledged my resistance to being more transparent, a palpable level of anxiety and discomfort thrashed around inside me. But this awareness and insight about myself became fertile ground for reshaping my understanding of transparency and how I might integrate it into my relationships with others. What I call reshaping was basically a shift in my understanding. I realized that confident people with integrated values do not fear being transparent. In fact, they feel more confident, less stressed, and more powerful—the kind of power I had observed in others that produced a calm and centered presence rather than bravado.

It was not hard to comprehend how this shift could affect my personal development and presence in the world. If I make it easy for people to know me, connect with me, understand my intentions and values—basically see my humanness—they soften their defenses and are more open to engage in a real way. Higher levels of mutual trust and confidence become the natural by-product of this shifting dynamic. An astonishing pragmatic benefit results: we collectively spend less time and energy jockeying for position around one another, which I personally find tedious and exhausting.

It Takes Commitment

Transparency does not come naturally to many of us. It's not a test that we set up and then pass or fail. Transparency is a capacity that we build and integrate into our way of being in the world, and it happens over time. We first become conscious of a gap in our confidence when we are with others. We experience fear, anxiety, and self-protection when vulnerable or exposed. We don't trust ourselves to be truly seen, heard, and understood. We eventually start to recognize the fallacy that our power lies in creating secrecy and subterfuge around things.

This level of awareness allows us to poke holes in our fears about being so vulnerable. We begin to let go of the worry that we might be taken advantage of, or worse, that someone might see something we don't like in ourselves. When we invalidate the epic narrative we've been carrying around, we make room for a new narrative to form about our power and confidence. When we challenge the perceptions, projections and scarcity thinking about ourselves and others, we then can create the mental and emotional space to reframe any situation to a more objective and clearer reality. The possibilities of that new reality allow us to connect with our confidence and self-trust. We then engage with others in a more open, more willing, and more transparent manner, which is another way of being versus doing.

I remember the day I acknowledged—with a sense of humor and lightheartedness instead of my regular anxiety and cloaked defensiveness—the reality that I am a flawed guy. I don't have all the answers, and being challenged is just part of the process so poetically called life and learning. On this particular day I was at a loss about how to deal with a significant situation—a tense dynamic with a client leadership team. The big aha moment came when I became open and completely transparent about the issues. No one reacted negatively or took advantage of my openness, and it didn't make me weak or inappropriately vulnerable. It actually lightened the load and gave me more confidence and credibility. My capacity for curiosity started expanding quickly in the moment, which gave me the confidence and support of the client team to work through the situation. When I walked away from the interaction, I was filled with a feeling of lightness and clarity rather than tension and confusion. I made a conscious commitment that day to continue developing awareness of when I avoid transparency in my life.

Curiosity is a powerful force that I believe further stimulates confidence, openness and a desire to understand, which are characteristics of authentic transparency. Curiosity suspends judgment and opinion. Curious people say to themselves or others, "I really want to understand this and see the possibility of something I can't see." Curiosity helps us put our own thoughts and feelings aside. It gives us great freedom in that we can be unattached in the moment and able to explore ideas with others. Curiosity allows us to recenter ourselves back to a place of confidence, which gives us easier access to authentic transparency.

By the way, curiosity is at the core of creativity and intelligence. Immense curiosity is a distinguishing characteristic of brilliant people. It offers fresh perspectives, a channel for new ideas, and diversity of experience. If you delve into the biographies of brilliant people, you will discover strong patterns of curiosity integrated into their lives.

Transparency is not something that can be forced. You can't moralize yourself or others into being transparent; it is something you consciously and courageously engage. Forced transparency is inauthentic, shallow, irrelevant and patronizing, which fosters feelings of self-doubt, resistance and defensiveness. Transparency is something that is invited, modeled and encouraged—never forced. Most people I've been around, regardless of their background, can sense inauthenticity. Even if they can't name it or articulate what is happening, they know when something is not real. I can't even count the number of times I've heard someone remark about another person's subterfuge or lack of genuineness.

Authenticity enables transparency to be powerful and influential. The intention to have integrity, be real and make genuine connections creates the possibility of something different emerging among people.

I was once with two colleagues in a presentation for a potential new client in Northern California. Generally presentations to prospective clients, for most professional-service firms or agencies, are really interviews, where you spend time promoting your credentials, experience and impressive list of previous clients. I decided to spend less time in self-promotion and talked about what it is like to work with us—literally the experience. I said, "I know there are any number of firms who can do smart and focused work with you, and in many ways, the technical and content aspects of what we all do is table stakes." I shared with the client that we have let go of the fear of ever being fired, which has given us the courage and creativity to engage our clients and never stand on ceremony. We believe this is what creates the best partnership and where the best work prevails.

As we were moving toward the end of the meeting, right before the conversation shifted over to the customary social banter, the VP of marketing said, "This was really an enjoyable time with you. We've met with three other firms. They all are smart and can clearly do the project. They present well and probably have clients that respect them. But you guys were refreshing. I feel like I know you. I feel like I really get how you work. You made it easy to see what you are really about." And then she said, "We will look forward to getting back to you." Wow, I thought. I said, "Thank you for sharing that with us."

As we left the conference room, I felt a strong sense of confirmation. I believed we would get the business, and I was jazzed. I was thrilled the VP stepped up and was reciprocally transparent, which further confirmed that it was a good fit. I was especially delighted that we were confident enough to be appropriately transparent in our presentation, so what really came through was something more than just our professional capabilities. The client experienced our confidence in who we are as people, not just as consultants (who we are versus what we do). We made it easy for the clients to open up and also be confident with us.

Developing Awareness

One of the steps for developing transparency is to allow it to have a voice. Giving something a voice is a powerful tool when we want to develop awareness and expand clarity, willingness and ability in any area of change in our lives. Giving something a voice enables us to get curious and ask questions, which in turn helps us understand where we have resistance and fear. Ultimately we then have an opportunity to shift.

In a previous chapter I mentioned the power of the question. Clarity and movement do not come out of an answer to a question but lie in the question itself and the dialogue that stems from exploring that question. When you give something within yourself a voice, it's the same as when you really listen to another person. You suspend judgment and projections and listen for new insights and truth.

Try giving transparency a voice. Ask yourself how and where you want to be transparent. Where do you feel the creative tension? Look at any resistance you are feeling—what's the fear? Giving it a voice by asking questions can help you understand the resistance and bridge the gap to develop new levels of confidence and trust in yourself.

There are questions you can ask to help you explore: What might people like to understand about me in this situation? What can I do to increase the connection here and inspire some courage—in them and myself? What am I most afraid to share in this moment or on this issue and why? What level of transparency would raise the confidence and trust in others? What do I want most in this situation that I'm afraid to request?

When I speak of "levels" with transparency, it's like adjusting the temperature in a room. Degrees need to be adjusted to get the room to the comfort zone, not just on and off. Discovering what level of transparency can create a shift in a situation allows you to respond authentically and confidently. For example, when I'm presenting to an audience and want the audience to connect with me and see me more than just a specialist on a topic, I engage a certain level of transparency that gives them insight into who I am—like a story, incident, or insight that lets them see into my humanness and realness. I become a person whom they are in relationship with during our time together.

Giving transparency a voice through your curiosity and exploration will provide clarity around how and when you resist it, as well as how and when you bring it forward. Clarity is about understanding what motivations and intentions drive you and influence the choices you make on transparency. Clarity shows up in the body as feelings of calm, centeredness, confidence and a heightened level of awareness. Lack of clarity feels unsettling, reactive, defensive, anxious and unfocused. A capacity for clarity, which can come through simple questions, gives significant insight about how to show up in any given situation.

Everything we've explored in the previous chapters elevates to a level of clarity and mastery with this principle of transparency. The experience of influencing others becomes more powerful when you exercise transparency and allow them to see who you are. You also set an example for how others might show up in the world when you rise to this level of clarity, confidence and integrity. People naturally gravitate toward joining you. They are pulled into a connection with you when you model transparent intention and presence.

Basically, by displaying transparency, you make it safer and easier for others to step into their own transparency. There is nothing for anyone to push against, fight, defend, or manipulate.

Tips for Your Development

Where does anxiety come up for you in relation to transparency? Name it. What is the specific fear? Name it. What stories have you created that feed the fear? Identify them. What might happen if those stories weren't true?

Over the next week look for every opportunity, personally and professionally, to step forward with a new degree of transparency. You will recognize these opportunities because you will feel the anxiety and desire to pull back. Instead step forward with courage and clarity, which will rally your confidence.

8

CHOSEN VULNERABILITY

RACHEL WAS A client with whom I had been doing professional-development coaching, and I had been seeing her for about six months when she sent me an e-mail, asking if she could get additional time in her next session. Something felt weighty and was most likely making her anxious, so I was happy to oblige. Rachel had been the clinical director over a system of subspecialty clinics for the past five years. When we sat down to talk, she told me she and her fiancé wanted to move to Denver. She continued to explain how much it meant to them to make the move. It was palpably clear this had been considered at length, and she had made a decision—they were moving to Denver. I said, "Congratulations. When's the move?" She sighed. "Oh wow, I don't know." Rachel went on to talk about finding a balance between looking and interviewing

CHOSEN VULNERABILITY

for a position while working in her current role. She feared the executive team would find out about her plans before she knew where she was going.

Rachel started down the path of what-ifs and then caught herself. She paused and said, "I don't want to be dishonest with my group."

I said, "Let's back up for just a moment. Are you excited about your plans?"

"Yes."

"Have you given this a lot of thought?"

"Yes."

"Do you think the clinic will fall apart if you leave?"

"No."

"Do you want the clinic to continue to do well after you leave?"

"Absolutely. Of course."

"Are you doing anything that lacks integrity in your decision?"

"No, I'm not."

"Would you like to help the clinic leadership through your transition?"

"Yes, I really would like to help select the next director."

I paused and then said, "Now let me ask you another question. What is it that you are afraid of?"

Rachel looked down and then up and said, "I'm afraid they will be mad and might just fire me."

I smiled and said, "Do you really believe that, or is that fear talking?"

She didn't hesitate when she said, "Fear. I feel really vulnerable."

I said, "Great. You're pushing those wonderful boundaries now and getting real." I then said, "Isn't it actually more likely that they will be sad versus mad?"

She blurted out, "Well, actually that's what I'm concerned about. I don't want them to think I haven't appreciated and enjoyed being there."

I said, "Great. Now stop being passively nice and be real."

We then talked about the level of respect and trust that she would convey by letting them be a part of the process since her move would impact them. This openness is a reflection of the integrity in the partnership she has had with the leadership team. Having the confidence to step into the truth and be appropriately vulnerable does not put her at a disadvantage but rather a profound advantage as she invites her colleagues into a circle of integrity. I pointed out that if she was transparent, she would open up a lot more possibilities than she would if she kept this a secret. She asked how I thought she should tell the leadership team. I flipped it back and asked her how she thought she should tell them. She said, "I want to sit down with all of them together."

I said, "There you go."

After three days I received an excited voice mail from Rachel. When I called her back, she said she couldn't wait until our next session to tell me how the meeting went. They were sad to see her go and wanted to know if there was anything they could do to keep her. They talked about different compensation: a sabbatical and letting her add someone to her staff to lighten the load. They even offered to connect her fiancé to some professional contacts if that would be helpful. She said she was overwhelmed but explained to them that she had decided to leave. They appreciated her trust and confidence in them, and they set up a session to work on a transition plan. They asked her if she was willing to leave her departure date open until after they had agreed on a plan. She said, "Absolutely." Two days later, when Rachel arrived for her session with me, she said, "You won't believe it. Matthew, one of the clinic partners, is going to introduce me to a network of his colleagues in Boulder and Denver."

Although the subject of vulnerability is core to the topic of this book and innately woven through all the principles, especially the previous chapter on *transparency*, I'm focusing on the topic in a small chapter here so you can identify and explore this very rich human experience.

Vulnerability conjures anxiety in most people. It raises some of our deepest fears of being taken advantage of, or worse, that somehow we are insignificant compared with others. Irrational as it may sound, the mere thought of or reference to vulnerability can make people feel like they are in a life-or-death situation. I use the term *chosen vulnerability* when I discuss this topic to give context for what I'm focusing on and to ground it in the intention of choice, which is the place where we trust ourselves and our self-worth to intentionally show up and fully engage our authenticity and humanity. Yes, it is true we can be physically vulnerable to an accident or illness or any other form of catastrophe. Our bodies are vulnerable to the aging process and viruses, our homes to earthquakes and fires, our neighborhoods to crime and fluctuations in property values.

However, as modern-day humans, we tend to project our general fears of vulnerability on all aspects of our lives—our identity, competency, reputation, and self-worth. We then create fabricated stories about how exposed and vulnerable we would be if people knew too much about us or knew the truth.

These narratives come out of past experiences—things we've heard, been taught, or conditioned to believe. More often, when the narratives are taken apart, they don't carry much relevance today, in the here and now, because their shelf life has expired. It's important to not judge or moralize these fear-based projections but to see them for what they are: narratives of distortion that are only as real as we choose to make them.

I've taught many learning labs on conflict resolution, and one of the modules in the course focuses on how to recognize your own defense mechanisms. What are the conditioned ways you defend and protect yourself against conflict? Understanding your fears of conflict helps you recognize your defenses. Eighty percent of participants consistently articulate that fear of failure is what paralyzes them and keeps them defended and not transparent. When I dig into the idea of failure, I generally find distorted and misplaced fear that is not based on any form of reality. The misplaced, pandemic fear of being taken advantage of or failing keeps you overly protected instead of engaged and showing up confidently with high degrees of trust. Confidence and trust enable you to choose appropriate levels of vulnerability so you can participate in more profound, authentic and transformational ways.

The Fallacy of Risk

Everything you do in your life that has substance requires you to be vulnerable so that you can fully engage the elements of learning, growing, expanding and flourishing. Falling in love means risking having your heart broken. Stretching in a new job means making mistakes and then being accountable. Pursuing a new sport means the potential of not excelling or at least sore muscles. Standing up for something you believe in means facing the possibility of others not agreeing with you. Life in all its brilliance means putting yourself out there—yes, in a position of chosen vulnerability.

Chosen vulnerability has the following characteristics:

o Grounded in self-trust and self-knowing, not based on fear and distrust
o Open and accessible, not passive and weak
o Aware and observant, not cautious and defensive
o Confident and assured, not insecure and suspicious
o Curious and explorative, not confused
o Operating from abundance, not from scarcity

Transparency puts us in a state of chosen vulnerability, which is how I describe the powerful and meaningful act of making an intentional choice. In other words, to be choiceful means to be in full clarity of intention. When we are around people who display this level of choiceful intention, they exhibit clarity and a sense of purpose. They have an ease, confidence and lightheartedness that are contagious. At the core they are not directed by anxiety and fear, although they are aware of it and can feel it. They understand anxiety and fear as expressions of their humanness, not dictates of how they should live. With this awareness, they recalibrate their reality with a deep trust in themselves, knowing that their chosen vulnerability never makes them fragile but, in fact, very powerful.

Our self-worth, character, credibility, and reputation are not fragile when we are intentional and choiceful in how we show up in the world. Make no mistake. No one tries to take advantage of this kind of clarity and strength of transparency. Cowardice is what tries to take advantage of a situation, and cowardice backs away from this level of presence.

As you explore your vulnerable place and your insecurity that lives within, look for your confidence that also lives there. This is the place where you will find your humanity and your brilliant courage and power.

Now go share the power of your humanness.

Tip for Your Development

The question, "What is your greatest weakness?" continues to be one of the most dreaded experiences during a job interview. For this exercise, however, answer it truthfully. Write a brief narrative about your insights on your greatest weakness. Just look at your insecurities. Ultimately your greatest weakness is actually the area you most want to develop. It's where you are still growing and evolving and where you want to build more confidence and trust. By the way, that's what an interviewer is really interested in hearing—your insights and authenticity, not your perfection or imperfection.

THE ART OF NOT KNOWING

I'M PERIODICALLY ASKED to step into a substantive session with a client, like with the following one, where I don't have a history with the client and not much of a backdrop on their business or insight on their dynamics as a group. These situations can create a certain level of anxiety for me. To be honest, it's performance anxiety as the expectations are usually high from the client, and I'm walking in without much context or backstory. Bottom line, I have to show up and suspend what I think I know and embrace the confidence to be open to the direction that needs to unfold. When I approach it this way, I can get to the core issues and help the client get clarity much faster.

A new client asked me to facilitate a three-day strategic retreat with the organization's innovation and technology division. The leadership members brought their teams in from around the world to help strengthen alignment throughout the division and, they hoped, develop a more aspirational approach in the way they focused on their consumer categories.

By midmorning on the second day, clarity unfolded for me around the dynamics of the group. I pulled the three divisional leaders aside to share some insights about the group and talk about direction for the remaining time together. I observed a bright and experienced group of people playing it safe—basically rehashing everything they knew. When ideas were raised in the group, they were explored through an old, outdated filter. It was like the group could only surface stories of what had always been. I told the leadership team, "I've not heard one word of curiosity, questioning, or probing—it's a bantering of what they each know." The three leaders sat there and didn't say a word for several seconds. As I sat in silence, I waited and hoped I had pushed the boundaries. Charles, the least senior of the three, spoke up, "I totally see it and probably would have walked out of here on our last day, frustrated by our lack of progress, and not even know why."

Gretchen, another member, agreed and asked me if I thought they, the leaders, contributed to the pattern and what I would suggest going forward.

When the session reconvened, I went full-on transparent and gave the group my feedback in the form of a story. I told them what it was like for me coming to the retreat, how I had to suspend everything I knew to be able to be open to discovery with them. I shared my observations of the group and the feedback I had given the leadership team. I then said, "I'm not going to tell you what to do, but I will help you explore the direction you want to go."

I thought I might get some debate from the group. What I got instead were questions and comments of awareness and some embarrassment. There were remarks about their current dynamic not being an acceptable way for them to run their business and that it was not reflective of an innovation-technology team. There also was some sobering dialogue about all the ways this pattern showed up from the way they research and design to how they collaborate with marketing. I was seriously amazed by this shift in the group and the humbling effects it had on them. By the end of the retreat they created a framework for integrating more substantive consumer insights through a new approach using cross-disciplinary teams.

During dinner that evening one of the team members from Europe sat next to me and confessed he was feeling kind of upset. He said that during the afternoon's discussions he was reminded of the comments his wife made about him always having an answer for everything. "She has told me I never show any curiosity in discussions, but I always have an answer." He then asked me what I thought he should do. I told him, "Share with her exactly what you just shared with me." At that moment he was so real and filled with curiosity.

We live in a culture that has become misaligned with the idea of intelligence. So many people believe that "knowing is good" and "not knowing is bad." As a result, we often try to appear intelligent rather than actually being intelligent. We put on the pretense of knowing when we don't, or we hide out when we think we don't know something. And when we think we do know something, we make sure everyone else knows that we know.

There are so many perceived rewards for knowing and so much effort invested in resources to ensure that we do know. We believe that knowing is what's required for us to succeed and win. The words *intelligent*, *smart* and *bright* are used so superficially in situations today that it frequently sounds like a person's intelligence is a commodity—either you have it or you don't. We approach intelligence, a.k.a. "knowing," with competitiveness and an attitude of scarcity, which causes us to grasp at information to shore up the appearance of intelligence.

This competitiveness and scarcity thinking concerning intelligence is driven by fear of losing and is void of curiosity and desire for expanding one's thinking and awareness.

We have a deep, driving need to be seen as significant and adequate, to be valued and appreciated, and to have something to contribute. This need, and the corresponding anxiety or fear around it, can make us believe we have to prove ourselves or show we are worthy—in turn, causing us to buy into the various perceived tests in life.

We experience tremendous growth when we go into the world to see who we can be, what we can do, and how far we can go. Unfortunately sometimes we can get caught in that metaphoric "proving ground" that extends beyond the years we needed to learn to walk.

In a previous chapter I discussed scarcity and abundance mentalities. Being caught in this proving ground over time creates in effect a scarcity mentality about who knows

more and who knows best. Scarcity and abundance thinking become linked to our motivations on knowing. Scarcity
thinking in relation to knowing creates a need to survive
by gaining information rather than a desire for true insight
and intelligence.

Behavior patterns concerning who knows more and who
knows better can be found in our personal relationships,
among organizational leadership and divisional teams, and
in our political leadership. Over time these patterns create a trap that leads to a quagmire of mediocrity—filled
with noise and debate and rarely anything of sustainable
substance. However, we can shift these moments to be
transformative by engaging and elevating through courage,
clarity, brilliance and discernment to foster new discoveries,
innovation, change and resolution.

Don't Be Confused

The practice of not knowing needs to be distinguished from
chronic confusion and debilitating doubt. Nothing is virtu-
ous about confusion. The confused person is somewhat lost
and disconnected from life. Doubt causes the mind to be
agitated so that it contracts with hesitation and indecision.
Confusion and doubt create murkiness and obscurity in our

thinking and behavior. Confusion and doubt are generally unconscious, involuntary reactions to fear.

Not knowing simply means you are not limited by what you know. You can hold what you know lightly and with confidence, yet you are willing and ready for it to be different. Maybe it is this way, but maybe it is not. Not knowing, as a practice, becomes a choice meant to bring greater awareness, clarity, connection and trust. Not knowing does not literally mean you don't know. It doesn't mean you have lost capacity for remembering. It doesn't require you to forget everything you have known or suspend all interpretations of a situation. Not knowing is what creates the space for knowing.

In Zen philosophy, not knowing is referred to as beginner's mind. An expert may know a subject deeply yet be blinded to new possibilities by his or her preconceived ideas. In contrast, a beginner may see with fresh, unprejudiced eyes. The practice of beginner's mind is to cultivate the capacity to engage without preconceived ideas, interpretations, or judgments.

Developing the intention to use beginner's mind does in fact connect you to your deeper insight and higher intelligence. It also creates an environment that opens others' confidence and capacity to let go of knowing and join you in the exploration. You become the influence that raises the bar of brilliance in that moment. A Buddhist teaching says,

> *Difficulties come from thinking you know the answers.*
> *To clear one's mind of opinions helps make space for the*
> *spontaneity of what is trying to unfold.*

Fear of Criticism

The fear of not knowing and the fear of making a mistake are profoundly overrated and are in fact not the key issues. At the core of this dynamic is the fear of criticism. The fear of criticism is almost as common as the fear of death and just as damaging as the fear of poverty. The fear of criticism undermines a person's capability and development in critical areas of creativity, initiative, imagination and appropriate risk-taking. This fear takes us to an irrational space where we conjure stories of others' unsavory intentions toward us.

Let's take an honest look at what drives the need for appearances—the need to appear right, to appear that you know, and to appear infallible. We have a deep, wonderful desire to belong, to fit in, to be validated, and to be experienced as a person of value, meaning and worth. The undeveloped, egocentric and fearful parts of ourselves distort this need into a shallow and fragile need to look good where we are defined by others' meaningless approval.

The fear comes from a deep-seated, irrational aversion to rejection or being viewed as insignificant, where others have the power to decide our worth or even whether we are allowed to continue to participate in meaningful ways. Our early experiences of struggling to pass those tests in life keep the bogeyman of failure very much alive, just waiting around the corner to grab us.

When you understand criticism and acknowledge the disabling fear it can create, you will start to take real steps toward setting boundaries and challenging its efficacy. You also will begin to experience it in a more detached way, and you'll begin to notice that some people have large stashes of criticism they are quite willing to dole out to anyone willing to take it.

I want to be clear in distinguishing between the integrity of productive feedback, which is innately respectful and intended to support one's growth, and criticism, which takes on the veneer of "advice." In actuality, the latter is a thinly veiled dose of scorn and jaded negativity—that's why it rarely produces anything of benefit but rather invites resistance and mistrust.

A real breakthrough of this pattern will come when you recognize that people who are adept at handing out criticism have themselves been recipients of abundant criticism. It allows them to deflect their own fears and scarcity mentality of not knowing or not getting something right.

You never need to meet criticism with defensiveness, negativity or reciprocal scorn. Instead you can simply say, "Thanks, but the criticism (advice) is not really beneficial, and it makes it difficult for me to be open, explorative and trusting in this process. I would, however, be open to some respectful feedback if you have insights that would be helpful for me."

I've observed over the years that "knowing" something is frequently founded on a socially or politically constructed level of certainty rather than on actual discovered truth or insight. The disagreement of who owns the truth is not actually a discrepancy concerning the nature of the reality at hand but is really just a posturing for power and position—all out of insecurity.

The Advantage of Creativity and Innovation

Many industry-leading companies are making it a strategic priority to evolve their cultures to emphasize discovery over what they currently know, embrace new paradigms over existing ones, and drive change to unseat old ways of doing. They engage innovative methods to dislodge the cultural norms of siloed thinking and motivate people and teams to embrace more explorative thinking, curiosity, and cross-disciplinary collaboration.

Performance-management processes are evolving too. Instead of using the old metrics of measuring output, companies are developing awareness on the concept of being versus just doing. For example, we're seeing organizations that are open to new paradigms:

○ Ask more questions than they have answers for.
○ Focus on what people are learning instead of what they know.
○ Challenge things that don't make sense.
○ Fail faster and learn from it.

The ability to imagine new approaches, integrate new insights, and build better connections within groups of people comes from the willingness and ability to engage the ambiguity—the not knowing—which is part of life.

I remember when I personally found clarity on this dynamic of not knowing. I was giving a talk. I spoke for about forty-five minutes and then opened up the session to a question-

and-answer period. A gentleman in the audience asked if I would share some of my own personal learnings and insights about some of the issues I was talking about. I remember pausing for a moment to reflect on his question.

His question opened up a subtle new clarity in me. I looked at the audience and said, "I've never acknowledged this publicly before, but one of my significant insights is that I used to be very impressed with what I knew—always making sure that people understood my experience and my intelligence—and now I'm awed by what I don't know." I went on to share, "I've never felt more intelligent, had more curiosity and creativity, and it feels like my intelligence keeps developing. I experience a more relaxed level of confidence in most situations now, and the real bonus is how it decompresses and centers the other people I work with."

The anxiety of thinking I need to know has not gone away completely, but it is now easy to recognize in the moment, and I know it's related to insecurity about how I'm going to look. When I recognize it, it usually makes me smile or laugh. Socrates framed this up nicely for me: "The only true wisdom is in knowing you know nothing."

The Shift

Recalibrating oneself from appearing intelligent to *being* intelligent may be driven by any number of motivators. You might take this step because you desire a more authentic way of showing up. You may desire richer, more meaningful connections with people. You may be motivated to access more creativity and discovery. To mobilize this recalibration, we must align ourselves with conscious intention—uncompromising clarity, confidence, and genuine curiosity. This shift permanently alters the way we pursue intelligence because we start to see and experience a broadening and deepening of our capacity for accessing real intelligence, which I believe is where we access our wisdom.

Wisdom can never be completely captured. However, I believe it is important to establish what wisdom means to you. For me wisdom is the ability to integrate knowledge and information into choice. Wisdom reflects the values and principles that we apply to our knowledge—what we know. Simply put, wisdom is knowledge and information shaped into a decision through the application of principles or values.

The essence of wisdom is discernment, a keenness of insight and judgment. It's discerning ethical from unethical, helpful from harmful, truth from delusion. It's knowing when to act and when not to act. Discernment is what delivers the brilliance of knowing and elevates it to influence—the influence that emanates below the waterline.

Tips for Your Development

Here's one of the best exercises I've found on knowing: Think about your capacity for knowing as a whole pie. One sliver is what you know, and another sliver is what you don't know. The rest of the pie is what you don't know that you don't know. That last large piece offers a profound territory for exploration, with much to be discovered. Rather than be struck with anxiety because of it, try to see it as a wonderful opportunity to grow, expand, learn and develop. You are not a finished product, so enjoy every slice.

In an effort to raise your awareness of this concept—and awareness is critical—watch for what comes up for you in the moments when you think you should know or are supposed to know something. What is your greatest concern or fear? Name it and then identify the scarcity belief you carry around that fuels that concern or fear. Now step into your courage to explore the possibilities outside that thing you thought you needed to know. There is a whole level of truth and clarity waiting for you.

Here's an easy way to develop the courage to step into the space of not knowing. Before giving an answer to something, pose some questions of curiosity, exploration and further discovery to see what else you can find out that you didn't know. The core of your purpose is to find out more of what you don't know rather than reiterate what you already know.

Just for fun, watch and listen to yourself and others when someone says, "I know." What is it that you or they know?

Imagination is more important than knowledge.

—Albert Einstein

10

POWER OF THE STORY

If you don't know the trees, you may be
lost in the forest, but if you don't know
the stories, you may be lost in life.

—Siberian Elder

S HARON, THE PRESIDENT of a medical-technology company, stood in front of the engineering and marketing divisions of her organization just thirty days after the company merged with another technology firm. She was passionate about the need for the teams to come together in a unified and committed way to truly leverage the strength of the merger and the common mission. Without working toward a sense of unification, they would just be separate groups of teams protecting their turf and history. Rather than strengthen their position in the industry, they could actually erode it. Sharon started her meeting with the following:

"When Einstein was fifty years old, he was working on a unified field theory. Understanding unified field theory in layman terms, he worked on a theory that would frame the entire universe in a mathematical equation. As you sit with that concept, you might imagine how he had the attention of the global scientific community. Reporters hounded Einstein for interviews, and many camped all night outside his home in hopes of getting a crack at the story. Although Einstein liked sharing with the scientific community, he did not seek the public spotlight and frequently would avoid requests for interviews.

"There was an exception to this when he allowed an interview with one reporter from *The New York Times*. Carr Van Anda edited *The New York Times* at the time. While reviewing one of the professor's manuscripts, Van Anda found a transcription error in one of Einstein's equations. What? A newspaper editor found an error in Einstein's math? Rather than being defensive and insulted, Einstein was impressed and glad to be interviewed by this editor. His behavior with Van Anda was exemplary of how Einstein went about life: He did not fear being wrong but saw it as the path for learning and discovery, and when corrected, he did not experience it as an insult but as the step to more clarity and truth."

Sharon paused then said, "All of you in this room bring valued experience. You are bright and accomplished, or you wouldn't be here today, and you each hold important truths. All of this can lead to new levels of success in what we do and where we are striving to go. However, it will be wasted if any one of us thinks we hold the whole answer and have nothing new to learn. This is what will divide us. It will make us less smart, less innovative, and less efficient, and it will make for an uninspired organization. Einstein's relaxed, confident and trusting attitude made it easy for people to care about him and to want to support him and his work. Make yourself proud and settle into the confidence of learning with and from one another."

Storytellers have shaped our societies, cultures, and the way we think for all recorded history. Every culture known to exist has had a strong storytelling element. Ever since our ancestors could first communicate, we have gathered to share our stories. We have passed along tales to understand creation, told tragic stories of lost love, repeated accounts of real heroism, and shared simple stories of family and community history. Stories or narratives have been shared as a means of entertainment, as a way to educate and preserve culture, and to instill character and moral values.

The power of story gives us the ability to communicate abstract concepts and ideas. Stories give the teller the influence to emotionally enter people's minds and hearts. A storyteller has the ability to initiate happiness or sorrow, trust or suspicion, apathy or energy, or any other emotion you can think of.

Stories are so inherent to our human experience that children in every culture crave stories, and when they can't access them, they will make them up.

Stories contain the threads that weave together our ideas and beliefs, frame our values, and connect us to our desire for discovery and meaning. Discovery and meaning are the elements that enrich us and create commitment in our lives.

The roots of teaching, religion, ethics and psychology all exist within stories. We use stories of heroic and ambitious public figures to spur the imagination and inspire others. Sports coaches use stories of struggle and triumph to rally the winning spirit among team members. Insightful and consumer-centric companies use a strategic and creative form of storytelling to connect with their customers to create the perception of shared values.

What Makes Storytelling So Important?

Everyone's lives are inundated and overmediated with information, data, directives, taglines and headlines. Instead of energizing us and creating connection, meaning, and inspiration between us, this information overload promotes chaos, confusion, disconnection and cynicism. We have developed behaviors with the way we communicate, collaborate and engage that could best be described as overly transactional, superficial and impatient. We operate in a zone of low-level awareness about what makes sense to others, what creates connection and meaning, and how to foster the fertile space to develop something different.

We usually are aware enough to know we want something different than what we are getting from our interactions, but we blindly keep pushing the same irrelevant noise at people, wondering why they don't respond differently or why the outcome doesn't change. I don't believe these patterns are intentional—people are frequently shocked when they recognize them. But as recipients of this transactional and superficial bombardment of noise and irrelevance, we become unconsciously patterned and culturalized with this communication dynamic. It reminds me of the tourist traveling in a foreign country and trying to communicate with a local who clearly speaks another language. The tourist seems to believe that if he speaks louder and just enunciates the same words over and over, somehow there will be a transformational breakthrough in connection and comprehension.

We all desire connection, purpose and meaning. We want to feel aligned with others and to have a sense of value related to our actions, to how we commit our energy and time. We want to believe in situations and people. We ultimately want to have faith because it is through faith that people are mobilized and inspired.

Faith?

By *faith* I mean a confidence-based trust or belief in the truth or trustworthiness of a person, situation or concept. Faith is formed through stories and strengthened through experiences. It's what mobilizes the human spirit and energizes the mind to what is possible.

Meaningful narratives that trigger people's imagination allow them to reach their own insights and conclusions. These stories create faith and connection, stimulate inspiration, and mobilize change. People commit to and embrace ideas they understand and can see themselves being a part of. Telling a story that inspires your listeners means you have created something meaningful. It becomes real for the listeners, and they can see themselves in the story or relate to elements of the story that create connection for them.

The power and influence of a genuine story or narrative, whether it lasts thirty seconds or sixty minutes, has the potential to unlock and rally the aspiration and possibility in others. When others open to the possibility of something new or different, they tap into a level of energy, confidence, and empowerment, which your formal power alone could never create. This kind of influence goes beyond getting people to do what you want them to do. People actually exceed your expectations because they are inspired and activated by making your aspirations theirs—they pick up where you left off. Stories create relationships with people that transcend the rationale; they connect *below the waterline* to who they are.

Stories offer an invitation to your listeners—an invitation to see something different, explore something new, imagine something not yet imagined, or commit to something not yet committed to. An invitation taps into a natural form of abundance in others. Stories bring down walls and build connection, especially when you put your listeners in the story and make them a successful part of it. You can dictate, legislate, and intimidate people into doing something you want, but what you will get at best is a mediocre level of commitment from them, along with apathy, distrust, and resistance—oh yeah, and a healthy dose of politics too.

Everyone Is a Storyteller

The idea of storytelling is intimidating to many people. They feel like it is a skill or a gift of writers, actors, and professional speakers, but not something they can do. Some people get overwhelmed with the idea of having to come up with a story and deliver it, which is why it creates anxiety.

However, I believe each of us is a brilliant storyteller. Let me pose an assumption: I wonder if you are not incredibly adept at taking a simple event from your professional or personal life and telling yourself a complex story about who a certain person is, what is motivating him or her, what it is he or she wants, and what he or she thinks of you. You literally create whole scripted stories in your head—probably enough to make a short film—and you do it in minutes.

If you can be so creative in the spur of the moment, I can assure you that with some intention, you can frame just about anything into a captivating narrative.

The Secret Ingredient

Be clear with yourself about your intention and the outcome you want to create/produce by telling a particular story. Your goal might be to entertain, teach, set a boundary, or connect with others and create meaning. If you are only interested in providing the facts and moving on, or if you feel like your interaction with someone is a meaningless transaction and doesn't warrant your efforts of engagement, then you shouldn't be surprised when others respond with disinterest and disconnection.

Put yourself on the receiving end of what you want to say (be your audience): What is it about your dialogue that seems relevant, interesting or compelling? How might it create connection, confidence and trust?

A story can be as simple as providing context for how you arrived at your idea, approach, insight or solution. It might be a reflection on a previous experience that gave you the courage, experience, or motivation to do what you are doing today.

When people ask me how I decided on my profession, I tell them the story of how the profession chose me at nineteen years old, when I worked for a global airline. I observed how I used my role and the experience with this large international company—kind of like a research lab— attempting to understand the consumers' relationship with the company and the dynamics, qualities, and strategies that made the company so successful. I observed in myself a deep desire to understand the why behind patterns and behaviors in the business world, not realizing at the time that there were professional disciplines focused in consumer behavior, branding, and organizational development.

The story continues from there of course.

Listeners

Who are your listeners? They are your colleagues, clients, stakeholders, staff, employees, family and even strangers. When they make your story theirs—meaning, they take it in and integrate it into their experience—your influence moves beyond you and requires little energy on your part to promote or feed it. It comes alive in the space of connection, faith, and imagination.

Stories activate something much more powerful than the rational brain. Stories tap into people's feelings and emotions, imaginations, aspirations and possibilities. Delivering facts, statistics, and information is a rational, commoditized transaction that neither activates people's imagination nor inspires trust and commitment. You give your listeners a level of confidence and clarity when you put them into a story.

In chapter 6, "Defining Needs," we explored how focusing on solutions can become a barrier to cooperation and commitment when the needs are not identified first. Stories are a powerful and creative way to connect your listeners to needs, which form the basis for solutions. Tell the story about your needs. What makes them significant? How did you get clear about them? When you connect people to your intentions and the needs that are important, you create context and meaning, which offers a path forward.

A Powerful Link for Leading and Mentoring

Over the years I have observed many leaders who don't grasp the idea that stories have a profound effect on people. Instead they bombard the people in their organization with facts, demands, and solutions and then are surprised when they get resistance or mediocre responses. Using the power of narrative rather than data and analytical facts could elevate much of what many leaders aspire to accomplish with their organizations, stakeholders and boards. When you look into what makes successful companies today—organizations that have an energized and highly committed culture—you will see leaders who understand the power of mobilizing people with an aspiration and direction that connects them through a narrative. The aspirational energy and personal empowerment in these organizational cultures become bigger than the individual leader. These are the companies that know how to innovate, adapt, change, and have fun while doing it.

Stories Are a Powerful Influence in Children's Lives

Parents who understand they don't rule the hearts and minds of their children see they have been given the honor to help guide their children's views of themselves as well as how each will emerge in the world. Children are best nurtured through the use of stories, which can help them cope in difficult times and better understand their feelings. Stories create connection for children and help them feel less alone by showing that someone else has had a similar experience with their own. Also profoundly true for adults.

Stories help build confidence and self-esteem by creating context and giving kids insight into who they are and how they fit into the world. Stories stimulate the imagination and curiosity—both critical elements in developing intelligence—and they support language and communication development. The sharing of stories helps children bond and builds intimacy, but then stories do this for all of us.

I was attending a retreat in upstate New York and met a really cool couple from Boston. I was intrigued. They had their two teenagers with them, a fourteen-year-old son and a sixteen-year-old daughter. The couple told me over lunch, after I expressed curiosity about the kids being with them, that the kids asked to join them on the trip. (I've seen these wonderful family dynamics many times throughout life, and I'm always curious to discover these parents' attitudes and philosophies on parenting.)

After observing the kids and their interactions with their parents over several days, I finally asked the couple over dinner one evening about their approach to parenting. Did they have a specific intention when they thought about how they wanted to parent? "Very intentional and simple," Kate said. She went on to say, "Jeff [her husband] grew up in a rigid, abrasive, and authoritarian home, and it squashed the spirit of his three other siblings. He was the one who got out with a semblance of humanity. His siblings have struggled with stability in work and relationships, and the family overall is pretty splintered and doesn't have much connection with one another."

Jeff shared that when their children were very young he and Kate made a pact that they were going to raise the kids by creating a sense of curiosity and discovery and focus on helping them understand they had choice. He said, "Kate and I believe you have a small window of time in which you can set the stage for your kids. After that you have no real power, so we said, 'Let's not even start with power plays.

Let's treat them with respect and honesty and as highly functional little human beings—emphasis on the *beings*.'"

"How did you do that?" I asked.

"We always gave our kids context for things. We told stories and gave examples so that everything had meaning, even when we needed to keep it very simple. We always wanted them to understand where we were coming from and the values that were important. And now there is so much trust between the kids and us. We pretty much just offer counsel and suggestions, and we're there to love them and listen—it's fun."

Reminder

Stories should never intend to manipulate or deceive. Make no mistake about it, your audience or listener will know the difference between manipulation and engagement. People can innately sense manipulation even when they can't describe it. One of the characteristics of highly influential people is that they are always centered on their intentions. They know what they want to create, and they know the experience they want to leave others with. It has to be authentic.

Stories Are Frequently More Powerful Than Ads or PR

An airline was attempting to push wage cuts through its employee groups with the intention of creating a more financially stable company. A news story broke, exposing executives as propping up their own compensation packages while trying to cut the workforce's wages. Leadership attempted to use the old excuse of keeping senior leaders from abandoning ship, which further fueled toxic relationships within the labor negotiations. It finally became clear to the executive team, after widespread public condemnation, that they must also make sacrifices. By this time the impact of the story was embedded in the hearts and minds of its employees and parts of the public—their concessions were too little and too late.

A major tire company located in eight western states is famous for the stories of its founder. The stories usually reveal elements about his values and belief that if he treats his employees like owners, his customers will get treated with excellence. In one story it is late evening, and a car limps with a flat tire into one of the tire centers. The lights are out, and it is past closing time. The driver notices one of the employees getting into his car to leave. He waves the employee down and explains that he has yet two hundred miles to drive that evening. The employee says, "Let's get you fixed and on your way." The kindness and generosity this customer now raves about has hit the blogosphere, along with other stories of similar praise for the company.

What Is the Story You Want to Tell?

Passionate specialists on storytelling note that it is the oldest tool of influence and also the most powerful. Many stories resonate with key areas of our lives. Many stories influence, teach and entertain. I think stories that explore who I am, why I am here, and my vision or view of the future are especially significant because they help us create context and connection and also develop confidence and trust with others.

There are three questions you can ask yourself that will help you frame/develop your story:

Who am I?

At the core of every encounter where you hope to influence others or want them to hear and understand you, people will want to know who you are. Once people have a sense of who you are and what you are about—basically when you demonstrate who you are through narrative or story—your listeners will relax and connect with you. The story of who you are is one of the most important because it initiates transparency and accessibility and demonstrates a level of authenticity and confidence. It also allows people to see how interesting you are.

I was leading a four-day professional symposium that would put the participants in some pretty intense situations. It was necessary to build relationships and collaboration through the process. At the beginning of the session, when we were introducing ourselves individually, one guy really stood out. Rather than going through the linear facts about where he was from, what he did, and why he was there, he said, "I grew up as an insecure kid worrying about fitting in. I think I'm still basically insecure, but now I find it amusing when it pops up. Many people who know me would describe me as having a calm disposition, which hides a character that is spontaneous, adventurous, and has a capacity for silliness. I would tend to agree. And you should know, I like people who make me laugh and make me think." The group laughed and immediately relaxed after he spoke, and it was interesting to watch people engage with the same energy he exhibited.

Why am I here?

Telling this story lets you be a bit more specific if you have an agenda or goal or something you need to accomplish with others. In chapter 7, "Transparency," I outlined how solid intentions and sound goals, when connecting with people, helps remove any second-guessing or suspicion on the part of your audience or listener. People respect honesty and healthy ambition. They despise deception and exploitation.

Patricia stood in front of a high school assembly and talked about how she had left her job for a year to create a program for teens that would mobilize them to become activists against teen drinking and driving. She shared how her son and three other youths were killed in an auto accident caused by drinking and driving. She said that even as a good student and athlete her son was not immune to the pressures of teen drinking. "What makes this so painful,"

she said, "is it was not an accident. It could have been prevented." She then paused and said, "I can't change what happened, but I can appeal to every one of you in this auditorium because each of you can impact these kinds of events in the future."

What is my vision or view of the future?

This story is generally told after your audience knows who you are and why you are interacting with them. Why should this audience, individual or team commit their time, money, energy or support to your vision? Providing a list of facts and reasons is not enough to bring them on board, and this approach may create an unappealing dynamic that will further disconnect your listeners. The vision story helps you connect with people around the value of your vision. How will people find value in your vision and want to commit to it themselves? Where can they make the vision theirs?

A note about vision stories, these stories can work through the written word. However, they need to activate people's feelings and values through context and meaning to create the connection and possible commitment to go on the journey with you. Whenever possible, people need to hear these stories directly from you, and they need to feel the experience. If it is important, then I say, let your audience see the whites of your eyes and hear the tone of your voice.

A CEO for a health-care system was feeling extremely passionate about the direction and goals he and his leadership team had identified for the next three years. His passion had been ignited further by the story of Richard, one of the organization's patients, who exemplified the power of their vision. What drove the CEO was how broken health care was in the United States. He believed that his team had to exhibit the courage of the organization's founder 150 years ago when she was an agent of change. He said, "I have to tell the story of how we got where we are today and where we are going and why we are going there, and I have to tell people in person." He took his vision and a film of Richard telling his story on the road and met with all the facilities in the system. He knew he needed people's full engagement and commitment to make this vision real and not just a temporary feel-good moment.

I like the way Robert McKee describes stories as the "currency of human contact," where they creatively convert life into a more meaningful and powerful experience.

Tips for Your Development

o Pay attention to how many stories you are already
   telling as you go about your day.
o Over the next week look for opportunities in which
   you might normally communicate to a person or
   persons with data and facts. Instead deliver that
   information as a brief narrative or story to create a
   completely different experience. Give the information context, texture, personality and a voice rather
   than presenting it as just facts. It may be as simple
   as sharing with them what you went through in your
   own discovery about the facts and data.
o When thinking about a story or narrative, ask yourself two simple questions: What is my intention in
   this situation? What is my intention with this person? Be honest and clear so that people understand
   and connect with your intentions. You can actually
   state your intentions. This is great practice, and it
   really will build your awareness of transparency.
   What would you like people to walk away with after
   interacting with you?
o Don't get overwhelmed with the idea of assuming
   the role of storyteller. Keep it easy. Tell your listener a
   brief story about what motivated you to be there and

what you hope to see happen and why it is important. Think of what got you excited about the topic or issue and tell them a story about that.

AFTERWORD

I DON'T BELIEVE that life is a test—a silly joke that divine intelligence put in our way to navigate with awkwardness and stress. I believe that life is about discovery, expansion and experience, and this happens through all the amazing senses with which we've been endowed. Life is intended to be an adventure seasoned with some challenges. Those challenges aren't good or bad, but they do create the diversity of experience that allows us to expand awareness and sense of self while we deepen our capacity for growth and connection. Those challenges show us what we are made of—who we really are.

That expansion allows us to live more fully, more creatively, more brilliantly, and more abundantly. We don't have to go searching for the meaning of life; we give our life meaning.

Life offers a proposal for full and conscious participation. It asks us to step up and engage, put our skin in the game. Of all the challenges we face, the greatest one is actually conquering fear and embracing the confidence to be fully present, pursue our aspirations, and walk our values—to make meaning.

The old type of courage involves a lot of heavy lifting to try and force yourself through the fear and anxiety to do what you need to do. You judge the situation and put expectations of success or failure on your ability to navigate through it. Another form of courage is when you open to your own capacity for compassion and respect for yourself in the fear space. It's when you give yourself permission and support to move through and beyond it without judgment, force, or criticism but rather with curiosity, determination, and play. The fear doesn't disappear instantly, but its ability to control and dominate your behavior, intention, and experience shifts.

Consider the fear-based parts of yourself, the areas where you've created unconscious, protective patterns that help you function in the world. Moving through your fear in these areas allows you to resolve, rebuild and rewrite your story. The new story is filled with fresh possibilities. These aren't sentimental and romantic gestures but solid, intentional foundations for real growth. Don't avoid these areas of discovery because of anxiety but rather explore them with curiosity, compassion and confidence as they are yours for the taking. Maya Angelou said,

Courage is the most important of all the virtues, because without courage you can't practice any other virtue consistently. You can practice any virtue erratically but nothing consistently without courage. One isn't necessarily born with courage, but one is born with potential.

A commitment to engage and live courageously does not eliminate fear and anxiety; however, it does give you the clarity, confidence, and discipline you need to move through fear with much more ease and effectiveness. Then the distortions, projections, and old narratives that house your fears start disappearing, and a whole new reality opens to you. This is the definition of fearlessness. It is the place you will feel awake and very alive.

Remember, nothing needs to be fixed; it needs to be awakened and developed.

I've distilled the concepts and principles from each chapter in this book into the following insights. For me these insights represent personal commitments I've made for how I intend to show up in the world. The great thing about these commitments is that they can apply to everyone and every situation I encounter, both personally and professionally. They can become a personal charter for you as they have for me. When I miss the opportunity, for whatever reason, to engage from my values and commitments, these insights give me the awareness to recognize it, understand the situation, and then clean it up. It's never about perfection; it's about intention and choice.

Insights

- You have one of the greatest powers: choice. Every day you are presented with large and small opportunities for conscious choice, and you can redefine reality in those moments.
- All people want to be treated with generosity—meaning, they want to experience respect and humanity in a similar way that you want. You can take it a step further and engage people using the platinum rule: treat people the way they want to be treated.
- People want to understand. People need to have context and understand the meaning behind situations that impact them or things that are asked of them. People don't commit or put energy into things that don't make sense. You wouldn't; why should they?
- People, regardless of their life experience or education, know when they are being manipulated, forced, and coerced, so don't think that your good looks or intellectual prowess is actually winning them over.

- Transparency is one of the most powerful intentions or behaviors you can foster. People move into a place of trust when something is real, and they can see what it is. Don't let your ego fool you. Appropriate transparency is real power. Secrecy and manipulation stem from fear and cowardice.

- Everyone likes to feel understood and relevant. Take time to hear who he is, what concerns her, and what they have been thinking about. Make an effort to validate who people are and whatever experience they had or have.

- People like to feel smart. Let go of your insecurity that there are not enough kudos to go around. Allow other people to be smart. Your IQ will go up multiple points in others' minds if you are the one who creates space for their intelligence and creativity to emerge.

- People like to be part of the solution, even if they don't get to make the final decisions. They like to be asked and included, and that inclusion is what motivates others to commit.

- People love to be successful. There is plenty of success to go around. Allow others to shine.

- Know the difference between being political and being politically savvy. *Politically savvy* means operating from a place of awareness and acumen. *Political* means operating from a place of fear and manipulation.

○ Remember, it's the experience with which you leave people—how they felt with you—not the facts, that will be the basis of the narrative they use to describe you.

For Practice

Many of you may want to develop some real traction around some of these principles, depending on what resonates with you most. Here are some suggestions:

○ Write a personal aspiration or mission on how you see yourself showing up in the world. What does it look like? What does it sound like? How would you like people to respond to you? What areas of your life can you most easily see making this shift? Name three core areas where you will put your energy and focus into practice today.

○ Get a personal coach, mentor, partner or counselor. For some people a third party can help facilitate exploration in specific areas of development.

- o Ask a trusted friend or confidant to share beneficial feedback, observations or insights they have about you in specific areas.
- o If there is something you think would be beneficial to explore, trust your instincts and go for it. If you have further questions or comments, please drop me a note.

There are no magical points to leverage, no one book or workshop that will transform you, and no simple hidden tricks to master. Each of us must move into a deeply connected relationship with ourselves and embrace this wonderful space of discovery and personal truth. We frequently think it's the big ideas that really make the difference. Remember, all the big ideas are made up of small actions, conscious intentions, and choices.

I leave you with an invitation to push the boundaries of discovery to find what it means for you to move fully into the space of being. Being means becoming consciously choiceful, and in those moments when you are aware and connected to clarity, you will calibrate a level of power and presence that will tap into your brilliance. Here you can experience who you are below the waterline. You are the story you leave behind. Authenticity makes it memorable.

Courage and integrity make it transformational. What is that story?

Go play with these insights. Use them to explore and expand. Remember, don't judge. Have only gratitude for what you see, hear, and feel. Have fun, go hang out—live, work, and play below the waterline.

> *Flatter me, and I may not believe you. Criticize me,*
> *and I may not like you. Ignore me, and I may not*
> *forgive you. Encourage me, and I will not forget you.*
> *Love me, and I may be forced to love you.*
>
> —William Arthur Ward

APPENDIX

A witty saying proves nothing.

—Voltaire

MANY ASPECTS OF our personal and professional lives have become overly complex and unnecessarily difficult. We spend a lot of our mental and emotional energy navigating the complexities and challenges, which leaves us with little energy or focus left to enjoy the experiences and insights gained through these pursuits.

I believe that the real learnings—the insights that create a shift or change in how we see, understand, and engage with the world around us—are frequently straightforward and less complicated than we would like to think. Understanding this created a profound shift for me, a guy who has spent a significant amount of time complicating his life and struggling to learn how to show up authentically and powerfully in the world.

The quantity of information available to us today is immense and often overwhelming. Our challenge is not how to stay informed or be knowledgeable but how to extract and discern insights from the knowledge we gain and integrate them into our way of being. Insight and awareness are the catalysts that enable us to show up as discerning and intentional human beings. The quotes in this book are simple narratives I use to bookmark or trigger my awareness. They are thoughtful and profound reminders for how to be in the moment and how I want to show up.

Quotes frequently can be shallow filler for a void. They also can be the simplest form of insight to change a moment, a day, and a life.

Below is some brief background on the authors of these quotes and a simple reflection on what the quotes mean to me.

The privilege of a lifetime is being who you are. (Joseph Campbell)

Joseph Campbell (1904–1987) was an American contemplative researcher, writer, and teacher. He was gifted with an adventurous spirit, a deep, curious intellect, an open heart, and a passion for understanding the human experience. The vastness of his work was driven and influenced by the intersection of culture, religion, and mythology, and it spanned the fields of philosophy, psychology, literature, and art. The philosophy around his work is most frequently summarized by his phrase: "Follow your bliss."

The quote I included captures the clarity we all seek, which is our birthright and privilege. We want to be fully engaged and experience the rewards of joy, connection, and abundance, but often we are left disappointed, frustrated, and cynical because we come up empty-handed. When we become conscious of the fact that joy, connection, and abundance come from simply being, we can then start to experience the privilege of clarity.

> *Knowing others is intelligence; knowing yourself is true wisdom. Mastering others is strength; mastering yourself is true power. (Laozi, Tao Te Ching)*

The *Tao Te Ching* dates to the sixth century and is ascribed to the teacher called Laozi, whose name means "old master" and who was a contemporary of Confucius. The teachings are not religious in nature but are timeless principles for living, leading, and governing with morality, correctness, justice and sincerity. The parallel between these principles and the meaningful teachings of most great religious texts is quite profound.

This simple text from a lesson in the *Tao* exposes the fallacy and the conscious understanding of where true wisdom is found, as well as true power—the power that comes below the waterline.

> *The things we fear most—fluctuations, disturbances, imbalances—are the primary sources of creativity. (Margaret Wheatley)*

Margaret Wheatley (1941–) is a researcher and writer who studies the dynamics of organizational behavior. Her approach incorporates chaos and change theory and systems thinking. She applies these disciplines to analyze the development of leaders and learning organizations. Her work opposes highly controlled and mechanistic systems, which shut down creativity, innovation and change because they create robotic behaviors and rote outcomes. She is a contemporary educator and leader in the movement to manage the power of creative tension inside organizational culture.

If we can stay centered in the midst of change and anxiety, we will frequently be propelled forward with significant growth, new learnings and amazing opportunity.

There is no more destructive force in human affairs—not greed, not hatred—than the desire to have been right. Nonattachment to possessions is trivial when compared with nonattachment to opinions. (Mark Kleiman)

Mark Kleiman (1951–), professor of public policy at UCLA and author of *When Brute Force Fails*, is a passionate educator, advocate, and change agent when it comes to public policy and public leadership and their implications on society.

This quote captures the impact of lost opportunities, broken relationships and damaged trust when we engage the world around us from our biased projections and fear-based attachment to being right.

Shallow understanding from people of good will is more frustrating than absolute misunderstanding from people of ill will. (Martin Luther King Jr.)

Martin Luther King Jr. (1929–1968) was a pivotal visionary and leader for the burgeoning civil rights movement in the 1950s and 1960s. He took many of the ideals for his work from Christian teachings and his operational principles from Gandhi. King's vision, courage, and leadership on equality, justice, and peace challenged and changed core beliefs, attitudes, and behaviors in the United States and around the world. In this quote taken from his "Letter from Birmingham City Jail," King reflects on how the experience of empty, apathetic and lukewarm understanding is far more bewildering than the straightforward experience of outright rejection.

> *No law or ordinance is mightier than understanding.*
> *(Plato)*

Plato (approximately 429–347 BCE) is one of the most influential philosophers of his time. He was the most famous of Socrates's students and became the teacher of Aristotle. Plato's work blends the fields of ethics, politics, philosophy and moral psychology into an interconnected discipline of philosophy. His work has shaped the field of contemporary philosophy that we know today.

This quote emphasizes that laws or ordinances cannot parallel the power that comes from a place of understanding. You cannot legislate or control the power of understanding among people because it comes from a place of conscious intention.

The single most important decision any of us will ever make is whether or not to believe the universe is friendly. (Albert Einstein)

Albert Einstein (1879–1955) was a theoretical physicist and philosopher. He is considered by most as the father of modern physics. He is recognized not only as a brilliant scientist but also as an intellectual with profound originality. He was a deeply observant individual, and his brilliance is attributed to intellectual solitude. Exploring the intersection of science and philosophy gave him a profound thoughtfulness in his work, which is nicely reflected in this quote.

This quote, which is really a reflective question, poses a wonderful challenge: The basis of abundance and the ability to be open to the possibility of something different is the belief in something greater than oneself. Is it possible that the universe will conspire in your success?

Pessimism is rampant in cultures on their way out. (Friedrich Nietzsche)

Friedrich Nietzsche (1844–1900) was a German philosopher whose work influenced many other fields, including art, history and politics. He questioned the value and objectivity of the truth that was held by institutions of religion (Christianity) and traditional morality. He was not anti-morality or antivalues, but rather he was a supporter of "life affirmation." He was a proponent of the honest questioning and challenging of any doctrine that drains life's expansive energies.

His comment from the nineteenth century is quite relevant today. Pessimism and cynicism are powerful by-products of lost hope. People who have lost hope don't believe in the possibility of anything different from what currently exists. Ultimately pessimism and apathy become self-fulfilling prophecies.

> *I cannot give you the formula for success, but I can give you the formula for failure, which is: Try to please everybody. (Herbert Swope)*

Herbert Swope (1882–1958) was a journalist and editor who spent most of his career at the *New York World* newspaper. He was the first person to receive the Pulitzer Prize for Reporting. He also developed the op-ed concept for opinion pieces, which were printed opposite the editorial page.

He was known to make this comment from time to time. It underscores how honesty, respect, transparency and healthy boundaries create connections that promote trust and credibility. Appeasements undermine credibility, courage, and ultimately, trust.

> *Judge a man by his questions rather than by his answers.*
> *(Voltaire)*

François-Marie Arouet (1694–1778) is better known by his pen name, Voltaire. He was a prolific writer and philosopher during the Age of Enlightenment, an era in eighteenth-century Western philosophy. Proponents of this age advocated reason as the primary source of legitimacy to reform intolerance, religious dogmas, and institutions of the day. Voltaire was a passionate, witty, outspoken advocate on many aspects of social reform.

This quote is an example of his wit and insight, pointing to his observation on how people engage. Through curiosity and exploration, you make yourself accessible, and people connect with and understand you. Questions come from a place of curiosity and a desire to understand. Answers and statements frequently come from personal agendas and a desire to look good.

> *There are no secrets better kept than the secrets that everybody guesses. (George Bernard Shaw)*

George Bernard Shaw (1856–1950) was a playwright and literary critic. He was driven by a desire to challenge social injustice and the exploitation of working-class people. He examined the stark issues surrounding social problems and used dark comedy to make them more accessible. He was the only person to be awarded both the Nobel Prize in Literature and an Academy Award.

I believe this quote captures Shaw's humor and contempt for manipulation. Too often people and companies have the delusion that no one knows their secrets even though their behavior tells the true story.

> *Difficulties come from thinking you know the answers. To clear one's mind of opinions helps make space for the spontaneity of what is trying to unfold. (Buddhist Teaching)*

This teaching offers a way to connect to authentic power and real intelligence by using the capacity for exploration and discovery.

> *The only true wisdom is in knowing you know nothing. (Socrates)*

Socrates (469–399 BCE) was a classical fifth-century Greek philosopher and Plato's teacher. He is most widely recognized for his contribution to the field of ethics and the development of the Socratic method (a form of inquiry and debate designed to stimulate critical thinking).

This simple quote reveals the level of discernment required to understand the difference between the idea of knowing and true wisdom.

> *Imagination is more important than knowledge.*
> *(Albert Einstein)*

Einstein reflects on the power of curiosity, observation, and exploration as the path to real discovery and the qualities necessary for success. Imagination was at the core of his brilliance and success.

> *If you don't know the trees, you may be lost in the forest,*
> *but if you don't know the stories, you may be lost in life.*
> *(Siberian Elder)*

Siberian elders are respected teachers and leaders of aboriginal or native tribes in the Siberian region of Russia.

Stories allow us to create context and shape and give meaning to life beyond the facts, figures and descriptions that make up our contemporary lives. It is amazing how easy it is to create clarity and direction and align ourselves collectively through shared stories.

> *Stories are the creative conversion of life itself into a more powerful, clearer, more meaningful experience. They are the currency of human contact. (Robert McKee)*

Robert McKee's (1941–) storytelling path started as an actor at the age of nine in Detroit. His creative and influential career encompasses acting, directing, writing, and teaching. He developed the screenwriter's bible, *Story: Substance, Structure, Style, and the Principles of Screenwriting*, which has inspired many screenwriters today in the true art of storytelling, which goes beyond the mechanics of plot and dialogue. Although he is not credited for any produced screenplays, he is a teacher and coach of the craft. In 1983 he became a Fulbright scholar and began teaching his story seminar worldwide beyond the film and theater disciplines.

His clear vision that stories are the conversion of life into meaning and that meaning is the fabric of human connection could not be more relevant for us in the twenty-first century because we continue to seek meaning in every aspect of our lives.

*Courage is the most important of all the virtues because
without courage, you can't practice any other virtue
consistently. You can practice any virtue erratically, but
nothing consistently without courage. One isn't necessarily born with courage, but one is born with potential.
(Maya Angelou)*

Born Marguerite Ann Johnson (1928–2014), Maya
Angelou is considered one of the most visible and influential black female autobiographers. She was a writer, poet,
and teacher, known for her courageous, respectful, and outspoken position on many aspects of human and civil rights.
Her work weaves together experience, intellect, and heart
and is often used in schools and universities internationally. In recognition of her many contributions to society,
academia, and literature, she has been awarded more than
thirty honorary degrees.

This quote is especially poignant because every aspect
of Angelou's life has been a manifestation of courage. She
captures the core requirement for really growing into who
we are capable of being.

*Flatter me, and I may not believe you. Criticize me,
and I may not like you. Ignore me, and I may not for-
give you. Encourage me, and I will not forget you. Love*

*me, and I may be forced to love you. (William Arthur
Ward)*

William Arthur Ward (1921–1994) is an inspirational
frequently quoted American writer. A significant literary
contributor, he has published numerous articles, poetry and
meditations for decades.

This quote of Ward's captures the power of connection,
regard and love, which is possible in all of our relationships
when we are centered in our intentions—that space below
the waterline.

BIBLIOGRAPHY

Joseph Campbell Foundation.
   http://www.jcf.org. Accessed February 02, 2011.
Laozi. *Tao Te Ching*. Edited by Stephen Mitchell. NY, NY:
   Harper Collins, 1988.
The Literature Network. "Francois-Marie Arouet Voltaire."
   http://www.online-literature.com/voltaire. Accessed
   February 05, 2011.
Nobel Prize Foundation. "Albert Einstein–Facts."
   http://www.nobelprize.org/nobel_prizes/physics/
   laureates/1921/einstein.html. Accessed February 03,
   2011.
_____. "Martin Luther King Jr.–Biography."
   http://nobelprize.org/nobel_prizes/peace/laureates/
   1964/king-bio.html. Accessed February 03, 2011.
Spartacus Educational.
   http://www.spartacus.schoolnet.co.uk/Jshaw.htm.
   Accessed February 05, 2011.

Stanford Encyclopedia of Philosophy. "Nietzsche." Last modified April 29, 2011. http://plato.stanford.edu/entries/nietzsche. Accessed February 03, 2011.

———. "Plato." Last modified September 11, 2013. http://plato.stanford.edu/entries/plato. Accessed February 03, 2011.

———. "Socrates." Last modified March 19, 2014. http://plato.stanford.edu/entries/socrates. Accessed February 05, 2011.

UCLA Department of Public Affairs. "Mark Kleiman." http://www.publicaffairs.ucla.edu/MarkKleiman. Accessed February 03, 2011.

Ward, William Arthur. http://www.williamarthurward.com. Accessed February 03, 2011.

Wheatley, Margaret. *Leadership and the New Science*. San Francisco, CA: Berrett-Kohler, 1994.

Wikipedia. "Herbert Bayard Swope." Last modified October 07, 2014. http://en.wikipedia.org/wiki/Herbert_Bayard_Swope. Accessed February 05, 2011.

———. "Robert McKee." Last modified January 24, 2015. http://www.en.wikipedia.org/wiki/Robert_McKee. Accessed February 05, 2011.